herausgegeben von / edited by
Christiane Lange
Robbrecht en Daem architecten

MIES 1:1

Ludwig Mies van der Rohe
The Golf Club Project
Das Golfclub Projekt

2
Maarten Vanden Abeele, photographs of the 1:1 model

38
For one summer.
Preface and Acknowledgement
Christiane Lange

45
Ludwig Mies van der Rohe
Golf Club Competition, Krefeld, 1930
Sketches, Perspectives and Plans

62
Mies 1:1 The Golf Club Project
Christiane Lange

83
Michael Dannenmann *Mies 1:1* 2013

102
Figures in a Landscape
Paul Robbrecht and Johannes Robbrecht

116
Robbrecht en Daem architecten *Mies 1:1*

126
1:1, or: The Chasm of the Colon
Reinhard Wendler

136
Joachim Brohm *Mies Model Study (Golfclub) 2013/14*

152
Pictures in the Subjunctive Mood:
Models in Contemporary Art
Julian Heynen

170
Architectural Monument, Cultural Heritage,
and the Construction of Memory
Winfried Speitkamp

182
Thomas Florschuetz *Enclosure* (GC) 2013/14

192
It's about the Place
Christiane Lange in Conversation
with Alexander Schwarz

202
Author Biographies
204
Chronology of the Program
208
Credits, Colophon

209
Maarten Vanden Abeele, photographs of the 1:1 model

2
Maarten Vanden Abeele, Fotografien des 1:1-Modells
———

39
Für einen Sommer,
Vorwort und Dank
Christiane Lange
———

45
Ludwig Mies van der Rohe
Der Golfclub-Wettbewerb, Krefeld, 1930
Skizzen, Perspektiven und Pläne
———

65
Mies 1:1 Das Golfclub Projekt
Christiane Lange
———

83
Michael Dannenmann *Mies 1:1* 2013
———

103
Figuren in einer Landschaft
Paul Robbrecht und Johannes Robbrecht
———

116
Robbrecht en Daem architecten *Mies 1:1*
———

127
1:1 oder der Abgrund des Doppelpunkts
Reinhard Wendler
———

136
Joachim Brohm *Mies Model Study (Golfclub) 2013/14*
———

153
Bild im Konjunktiv.
Modelle in der zeitgenössischen Kunst
Julian Heynen
———

171
Baudenkmal, Kulturerbe
und die Konstruktion von Erinnerung
Winfried Speitkamp
———

182
Thomas Florschuetz *Enclosure* (GC) 2013/14
———

193
Es geht um den Ort
Christiane Lange im Gespräch
mit Alexander Schwarz
———

202
Autorenbiografien
204
Chronologie der Veranstaltungen
208
Bildnachweis, Impressum
———

209
Maarten Vanden Abeele, Fotografien des 1:1-Modells

For One Summer
Preface and Acknowledgement

Today, the Krefeld Egelsberg hill is a sea of blue lupin blooms. Nothing remains to remind us of the flat structure of wood and steel that stood for one summer, stretching far out into the landscape, attracting over 12,000 visitors.

In the middle of the lightly undulating landscape, a life-size architectural model was built on the basis of plans for a golf clubhouse made by Ludwig Mies van der Rohe in 1930.

Mies 1:1 The Golf Club Project was the name of the exhibition that consisted of a single exhibit and was initiated by the trust Projekt MIK e.V. in 2013 to commemorate the long cooperation between Mies and the Krefeld silk industry.

The Ghent architectural practice Robbrecht en Daem architecten took on the task of implementing Mies' eighty-year-old design as a 1:1 scale model.

The architects created an *objet d'architecture*, a manifestation of an architectural thesis that visitors could observe, walk through, and even listen to, particularly during the night, when the watchman's dog would prick up its ears whenever the wind whistled between the high-grade steel paneling of the columns or the tension of the wood was released with a crack reminiscent of a whip.

Initially the term "model" was simply a concept used to express that the intention was not to create a usable building in any traditional sense. Nor was the construction intended to appear as a usable building. Robbrecht en Daem architecten and I were completely in agreement about this from the beginning.

It was necessary for the project to distance itself from the tradition of the conventional architectural copy not only in light of the prevailing fashion of reconstruction, but also out of respect for Ludwig Mies van der Rohe.

Some professionals drew attention to the dangerous potential for failure, and rightly so. We were conscious that the quality of the result would not lie in transposing the given design on a millimeter for millimeter basis. On the contrary, in-depth research and an exact knowledge of the material offered in the plans were the prerequisites for moving beyond what was measurable and visible to the actual conceptual core of this unusual competition design, in order to develop a unique language for its first appearance as a kind of premiere performance.

Paul Robbrecht and Hilde Daem, together with their architectural practice, to which one of their sons, Johannes Robbrecht, belongs, are architects whose work is particularly marked by a proximity to art and artists. Having collaborated with them on an earlier project, I was familiar with their sensitive methods and their approaches that go beyond architecture.

It was their sheer excitement about even the vague idea of implementing Mies' Golf Club design as a 1:1 model that provided the incentive

Für einen Sommer
Vorwort und Dank

Heute erinnert nichts mehr daran, dass auf dem Krefelder Egelsberg, dort, wo jetzt ein Meer blauer Lupinen blüht, ein flaches, weit in die Landschaft ausgreifendes Gebilde aus Holz und Stahl stand und einen Sommer lang über 12.000 Besucher in seinen Bann zog.

Mitten in der leicht hügeligen Landschaft erhob sich ein lebensgroßes Architekturmodell, errichtet auf der Grundlage von Plänen, die Ludwig Mies van der Rohe 1930 für ein Golfclubhaus geschaffen hatte.

Mies 1:1 Das Golfclub Projekt hieß das Ausstellungsprojekt mit nur einem Exponat, das der kleine Verein Projekt MIK e.V. als Würdigung der langen Zusammenarbeit von Mies mit der Krefelder Seidenindustrie 2013 initiiert hatte.

Das Genter Architekturbüro Robbrecht en Daem architecten übernahm die Aufgabe, den mehr als 80 Jahre alten Entwurf von Mies als „Modell" im Maßstab 1:1 zu *vergegenwärtigen*.

Die Architekten schufen ein *objet d'architecture*, eine materialisierte architektonische These, die man anschauen, durchwandern und sogar hören konnte. Vor allem während der Nacht horchte der Hund des Wachmannes immer wieder auf, wenn sich der Wind in den edelstahlverkleideten Stützen verfing und das Holz seine Spannung mit einem peitschenartigen Knall entlud.

Der Begriff „Modell" war zunächst eine Hilfskonstruktion, die über das Ziel nur soviel aussagte, dass kein im herkömmlichen Sinne „benutzbares" Gebäude entstehen sollte. Und es sollte auch nicht wie ein benutzbares Gebäude erscheinen. Auch darin waren Robbrecht en Daem architecten und ich uns sofort einig.

Nicht nur vor dem Hintergrund der anhaltenden Rekonstruktionsmode war es nötig, unser Projekt von abbildhaften Nachbauten zu distanzieren, sondern auch aus Respekt vor Ludwig Mies van der Rohe.

Zu Recht wiesen einige Fachleute auf die enorme Fallhöhe unseres Vorhabens hin. Uns war bewusst, dass die Qualität des Ergebnisses nicht in der millimetergetreuen Übersetzung der Vorlage liegen würde. Eine profunde Recherche und exakte Kenntnis des Planmaterials waren vielmehr die Voraussetzung, um jenseits des Mess- und Sichtbaren zum eigentlichen Kern des Konzeptes dieses außergewöhnlichen Wettbewerbsentwurfs vorzudringen und eine eigene Sprache für dessen erstmalige Inszenierung zu entwickeln.

Paul Robbrecht und Hilde Daem mit ihrem Büro, dem heute auch einer ihrer Söhne, Johannes Robbrecht, angehört, sind Architekten, deren Werk von der Nähe zur Kunst und zu Künstlern geprägt ist. Mit ihrer feinen, weit über die Architektur hinausgehenden Denk- und Arbeitsweise war ich durch ein früheres gemeinsames Projekt vertraut.

Ihre Begeisterung für die noch vage Idee, Mies' Golfclub-Entwurf als 1:1-Modell umzusetzen, bot den Auftakt, das Unternehmen ernsthaft zu starten. Das war im Herbst 2010. Ihnen gilt mein erster großer Dank.

to start the project seriously. That was in the fall of 2010. I owe them a great debt of thanks.

Before opening the 1:1 model in May 2013, diverse prerequisites had to be fulfilled. David Chipperfield's assertion of architecture as a process, the success of which lies not only in the genius of the design but in successfully uniting the idea with all other accompanying requirements, regulations, expectations, and visions, was confirmed time and time again: "Architecture does not just happen … it requires collaboration."[1]

This collaboration was provided by the great number of people who cooperated in the realization of the 1:1 model: architects, static engineers, landscape planners, farmers, consultants, clerks of works, contractors, city employees and the local government, humanities scholars, journalists, lawyers, graphic designers, printers, translators, the members of Projekt MIK e.V., and many more who provided their abilities and their time, in part voluntarily without payment. Additionally, there were those who provided help during the project and after the opening by taking care of the place and the visitors, and organizing and running the numerous events that took place there.

In particular, *Mies 1:1* demanded constructive unconventional thinking, regardless of whether it had to do with the approval procedure, the provision of Internet access in the middle of a field, or the organization of a lecture in the 1:1 model while exposed to wind and temperatures of 13°. The project could have failed so many times, but solutions were always found. Perhaps it had to do with the "ephemeral joy" which one critic attributed to the project.[2] I wish to express my deepest thanks to everyone involved.

My third round of thanks goes to all the generous citizens and foundations who have supported our project financially. Through your contribution, you have lent your voice of support to a cultural project for which there were no previous role models or references, and which took place outside of the established cultural centers. There was no obvious guarantee of success. It demanded courage, and trust in the quality of the idea and in our work. I express my thanks in the name of Projekt MIK e.V. and all participants.

In the words of Paul Robbrecht on the day of the opening of *Mies 1:1*, "It was an intellectual joy to wander around the mind of Mies van der Rohe. Now, it is a physical and emotional joy, even a small miracle, to wander around the space conceptualized by Mies. Later it will be in our heads, in our memories."

With this volume, it is our intention to cultivate the memory of this great event. I thank the authors for their intelligent and knowledgeable contributions on the relevance of the model as an artistic strategy, as a template for thinking and building, and on the role of architecture as a source of memories. I also thank the photographers for their various ways of seeing.

Christiane Lange, Curator *Mies 1:1*, September 2014

1 "Architecture does not just happen, it is a coincidence of forces, a conspiracy of requirements, expectations, regulations and, hopefully, visions. It requires collaboration and its success is subject to the quality of that collaboration." David Chipperfield, text plaque at the exhibition *Common Ground*, Architecture Biennale, Venice 2012.
2 Kay von Keitz, "Mies erleben. Raum II: Ludwig Mies van der Rohes Golfclub", in: *Der Architekt*, No. 6, 2013, pp. 42–43.

Bis zur Eröffnung des 1:1-Modells im Mai 2013 mussten vielfältige Voraussetzungen geschaffen werden. Immer wieder bestätigte sich David Chipperfields Credo von der Architektur als Prozess, deren Erfolg nicht allein auf der Genialität des Entwurfs basiert, sondern in der erfolgreichen Zusammenführung der Idee mit allen begleitenden Anforderungen und Regeln, Erwartungen und Visionen: „Architektur passiert nicht einfach [...]. Sie verlangt Zusammenarbeit."[1]

Geleistet wurde diese Zusammenarbeit von den vielen unterschiedlichen Menschen, die an der Verwirklichung des 1:1-Modells mitgewirkt haben: Architekten, Statiker, Landschaftsplaner, Landwirte, Gutachter, Bauleiter, ausführende Firmen, Mitarbeiter der Stadt und der Bezirksregierung, Geisteswissenschaftler, Journalisten, Juristen, Grafiker, Drucker, Übersetzer, die Mitglieder von Projekt MIK e. V. und viele mehr, die ihre Kompetenz und Zeit zum Teil auch ehrenamtlich eingebracht haben. Zu ihnen kamen nach der Eröffnung diejenigen hinzu, die während der Laufzeit des Projektes den Ort und die Besucher betreuten und für die Organisation und den Ablauf der zahlreichen Veranstaltungen sorgten.

Von allen erforderte *Mies 1:1* konstruktives, unkonventionelles Denken, egal ob es um die Genehmigungsverfahren ging, einen Internetzugang mitten im Acker oder eine Vortragsveranstaltung im 1:1-Modell bei Wind und 13 Grad. Das Projekt hätte an vielen Stellen scheitern können, aber es fanden sich immer Lösungen. Vielleicht lag es an der „ephemeren Heiterkeit", die ein Kritiker dem Projekt attestierte.[2] Dafür möchte ich allen Mitwirkenden danken.

Mein dritter großer Dank gilt den Privatpersonen und Stiftungen, die unser Vorhaben finanziell unterstützt haben. Mit ihrer Förderzusage haben sie sich für ein Kulturprojekt ausgesprochen, für das es keine Vorbilder oder Referenzen gab und das außerhalb der einschlägigen Kulturzentren stattfinden würde. Es gab keine offensichtliche Erfolgsgarantie. Mut war gefordert und Vertrauen in die Qualität der Idee und unserer Arbeit. Dafür danke ich im Namen von Projekt MIK e.V. und allen Mitwirkenden.

„Es war ein intellektuelles Vergnügen, im Kopf Mies van der Rohes herumzulaufen. Jetzt ist es ein physisches und emotionales Vergnügen und auch ein kleines Wunder, dass wir in den Räumen von Mies herumlaufen. Und später wird es in unserm Kopf sein, in unserer Erinnerung", sagte Paul Robbrecht am Tag der Eröffnung von *Mies 1:1*.

Mit dem vorliegenden Band möchten wir diese Erinnerung weitertragen und kultivieren. Ich danke den Autoren für ihre klugen und kenntnisreichen Gedanken zur Bedeutung von Modellen als künstlerische Strategie, Denk- und Bauform sowie zur Rolle der Architektur als Erinnerungsspeicher. Und ich danke den Fotografen für ihre unterschiedliche Sicht der Dinge.

Christiane Lange, Kuratorin *Mies 1:1*, September 2014

1 „Architecture does not just happen, it is a coincidence of forces, a conspiracy of requirements, expectations, regulations and, hopefully, visions. It requires collaboration and its success is subject to the quality of that collaboration." David Chipperfield, Texttafel, Ausstellung *Common Ground*, Architektur Biennale Venedig 2012.
2 Kay von Keitz, „Mies erleben. Raum II: Ludwig Mies van der Rohes Golfclub", in: *Der Architekt*, Nr. 6, 2013, S. 42–43.

Förderer / Sponsors

    die Kulturstiftung des Bundes

    die Sparkassen-Kulturstiftung Krefeld

    und private Förderer / and private sponsors

Das wissenschaftliche Begleitprogramm wurde gefördert durch /
The academic programme was sponsored by

    Gerda Henkel Stiftung

    Goethe-Institut Chicago

    Stadt Krefeld

    Zentralinstitut für Kunstgeschichte München

    und / and Kunstmuseen Krefeld

Die Publikation wurde gefördert durch die / This publication was supported by

    Sparkassen-Kulturstiftung

    und private Förderer / and private sponsors

Mies 1:1 das Golfclub Projekt wurde initiiert und realisiert von /
Mies 1:1 The Golf Club Project was initiated and realised by

    Projekt MIK e.V., Krefeld

Konzeption und Realisierung der Ausstellung
Concept and realisation of the exhibition

Kuratorin/Curator: Christiane Lange, Krefeld
Künstlerische Leitung/Artistic director:
    Robbrecht en Daem architecten, Gent
Veranstalter/Producer: Projekt MIK e. V., Krefeld
Assistentin der Projektleitung/Assistant to project director:
    Britta Marzi, Krefeld
Veranstaltungsmanagement/Event management:
    Alexandra Lichters, Krefeld
Vermittlung/Education: Dr. Christiane Heiser, Köln
Presse- und Öffentlichkeitsarbeit/Press and public
    relations: Little Owl Film & Communication, Uedem
Kommunikation/Communication:
    Castenow Communications, Düsseldorf
Website: Heide von Berswordt-Wallrabe,
    Büro für visuelle Kommunikation, Bochum

Planung und Realisierung des 1:1-Modells
Planning and realisation of the 1:1 model

Konzeption, Planung/Concept, planning:
    Robbrecht en Daem architecten, Ghent, Belgien
    Paul Robbrecht, Hilde Daem, Johannes Robbrecht,
    Tom De Moor, Tine Cooreman, Thomas Hick
Projektsteuerung, Planung/Project management, planning:
    DGM Architekten, Krefeld; Dr. Wolfgang Melchert;
    Gerd Rother; Coskun Demirok; Veit Stolberg
Planung, Bauleitung/Planning, construction management:
    Architekturbüro Ruhnau, Issum
Statik/Structural Engineering:
    Ingenieurbüro Angenvoort – Kroth & Partner, Krefeld
Bodengutachten/Ground research:
    Geotechnisches Büro Dr. Müller, Krefeld
Vermessung/Surveying and alignment:
    Vermessungsbüro Roland Brockers, Krefeld
Erdarbeiten, Fundamente, Holzbau, Dach/
Earthworks, foundations, woodwork, roof:
    Grote Holzbau GmbH, Weeze
Stahlbau/Steel buildings: Schlosserei Fritz Beeser, Krefeld
Bodenarbeiten/Earthworks: Solbach Hoch- und
    Ingenieurbau, Viersen
Elektroarbeiten/Electric works: Elektro Stephann, Krefeld
Blitzschutz/Lightning protection: W. Wettingfeld
    GmbH & Co. KG, Krefeld
Überwachung/Security: Wachdienst Krefeld
    Wilh. Esters GmbH, Krefeld
Vorhang/Curtain: Ralf Ißel
Veranstaltungstechnik/Event technics: VPS Krefeld
Rekultivierung/Recultivation: Pieter Schwarze,
    Schwarze & Partner Landschaftsbau

Vermittlung/Education
    Katja Bernert, Karl Eick (Verseidag), Karola Goris,
    Rhoda Goris, Bernd Grau, Bruno Heinemann,
    Dr. Christiane Heiser, Cornelia Kesper, Christiane Lange,
    Filomena Lopedoto, Lisa Neupert, Robert Reichling,
    Jana-Catharina Rether, Sabine Sander-Fell,
    Sandra Schleuter, Rolf Schlue, Dr. Karin Thönnissen
Kasse und Haustechnik/Cashier and house technicians:
    Andreas Graeber, Brigitte Kox, Wolfgang Liedgens,
    Rita Linden, Veronika Möckel, Stephan Siebold,
    Klaus Trybul

Kartenvorverkauf/Ticketing: Eiscafe San Marco,
    Restaurant am Flugplatz Egelsberg,
    Mercure Tagungs-und Landhotel, alle Krefeld-Traar.
Dolmetscher/Interpreter: Franz Kubaczyk, Karin Walker,
    Nadine Hegmanns
Catering/Catering: Mercure Tagungs- und Landhotel,
    Krefeld
Buchhaltung/Accounting: thp-Treuhandpartner GmbH

Rat & Tat/Advice & Support: Hendrik Abrahams,
    Karl Amendt, Susanne Breidenbach, Noomi und
    Calvin Castenow, Ulrich Cloos, Peter Drecker,
    Heiner Engbrocks, Dr. Christian Fischer,
    Jörg Hallmann, Johann Heller-Steinbach,
    Dr. Martin Hentschel, Bernd Heuer, Dr. Julian Heynen,
    Thomas Janzen, Gregor Kathstede, Franz Kubaczyk,
    Helmut Lang, Rainer Leendertz, Stefanie Liedgens,
    Josef Limper, Martin Linne, Hannah Lorbach,
    Irmi Maunu-Kocian, Dr. Sylvia Martin, Clair Neidhardt,
    Martin Paniczek, Rolf Schlue, Dr. Christian Schmidt,
    Daniel Schröer, Claudia Schröer, Niko Schröer,
    Oliver Schröter, Piet Schwarze, Thomas Siegert,
    Carlheinz Swaczyna, Mic Thiemann, Heino Thiess,
    Volker Ulbricht, Dominik Weber, Peter Welling,
    Frank Werthebach, Adrian Wolff, Claus Ziegler

Filmteam/Film team

*Mies 1:1 Die Geschichte eines begehbaren
    Architekturmodells/
    Mies 1:1 The story of a live size Model*
HD 45 min D/E 2014
Buch und Regie/Script and director:
    Helge Drafz und Christiane Lange
Kamera/Camera: Bärbel Zibold
Kameraassistenz und Ton/Camera assistent and sound:
    Martin Schulze
Schnitt und Grafik/Cutting and graphics:
    Julius Krenz
Production: Projekt MIK e.V.

Model 1:1, Krefeld (G)
13 min 36 sec 2013
Regie/Director: Maarten Vanden Abeele
Kamera/Camera: Maarten Vanden Abeele
Schnitt/Image Editing: Gert Van Berkelaer
    mit/with Maarten Vanden Abeele
Tonschnitt/Sound Editing: Senjan Jansen/Senstudio
    mit/with Maarten Vanden Abeele
Drohne/Drone: Cammotion.be | Aerial Photo & Video
    Pilot/Pilot: Dirk Van de Velde;
    Kamera/Camera: Matth Mouling
Produktion/Production:
    Robbrecht en Daem architecten

**Ludwig Mies van der Rohe
Golf Club Competition,
Krefeld, 1930
Sketches, Perspectives
and Plans**

Ludwig Mies van der Rohe
Der Golfclub-Wettbewerb,
Krefeld, 1930
Skizzen, Perspektiven
und Pläne

Exterior perspective, 1930
Pencil on tracing paper,
8 1/4 x 11 1/2" (21 x 29.2 cm)
The Mies van der Rohe Archive,
gift of the architect

Perspektive, 1930
Bleistift auf Transparentpapier,
21 x 29,2 cm
The Mies van der Rohe Archive,
Geschenk des Architekten

Plan Sketch, 1930
Charcoal on tracing paper,
39 1/2 x 21 1/2" (100.4 x 54.6 cm)
The Mies van der Rohe Archive,
gift of the architect

Grundriss-Skizze, 1930
Kohle auf Transparentpapier,
100,4 x 54,6 cm
The Mies van der Rohe Archive,
Geschenk des Architekten

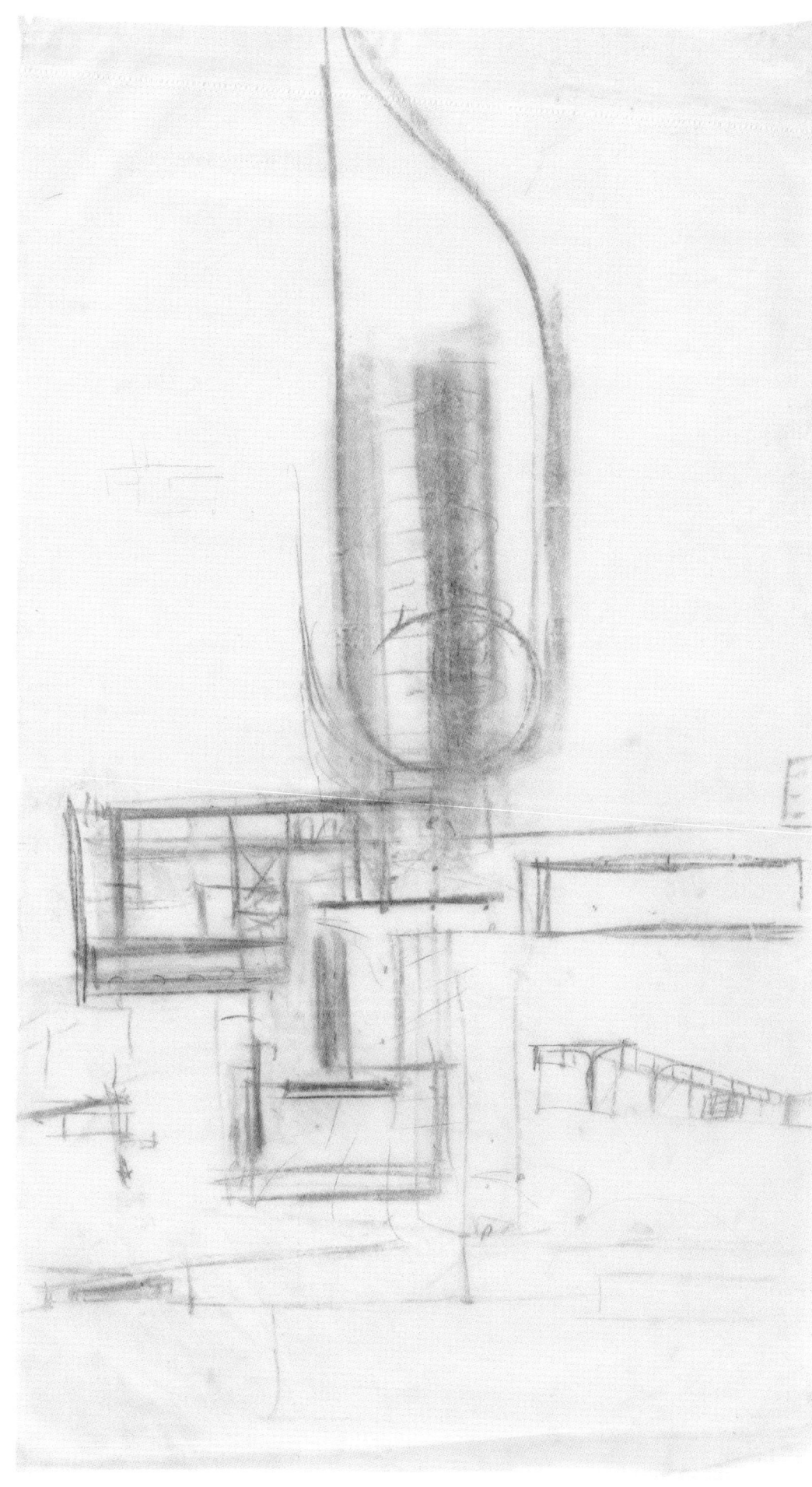

Exterior perspective, 1930
Pastel and Pencil on tracing paper,
39 1/2 x 21 1/2" (100.4 x 54.6 cm)
The Mies van der Rohe Archive,
gift of the architect

Perspektive, 1930
Kreide und Bleistift
auf Transparentpapier,
54,6 x 107,3 cm
The Mies van der Rohe Archive,
Geschenk des Architekten

Perspective sketch, 1930
Pencil on tracing paper,
21 1/2 x 36 1/2" (54.6 x 92.7 cm)
The Mies van der Rohe Archive,
gift of the architect

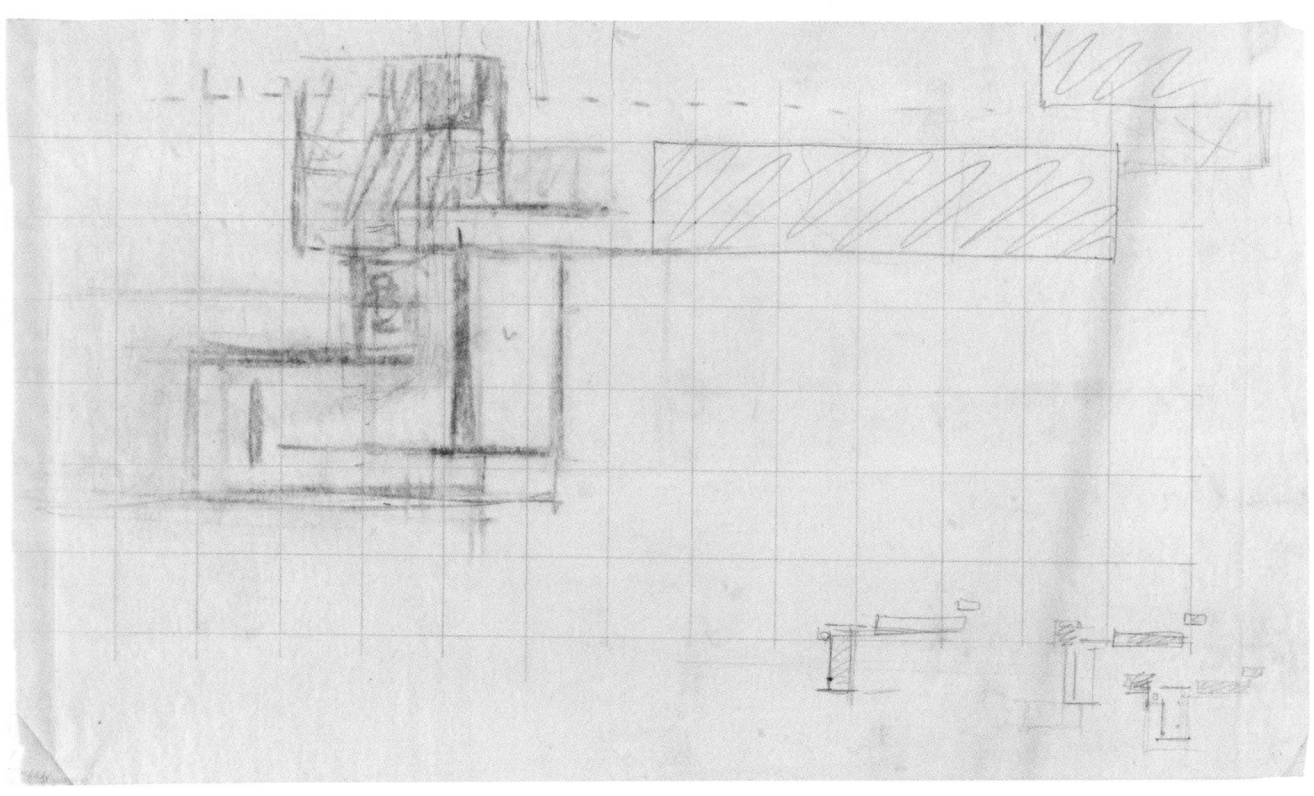

Partial plan sketch, 1930
Pencil on tracing paper,
21 1/2 x 21 1/4" (32.4 x 54.6 cm)
The Mies van der Rohe Archive,
gift of the architect

Grundriss-Skizze, 1930
Bleistift auf Transparentpapier,
32,4 x 54,6 cm
The Mies van der Rohe Archive,
Geschenk des Architekten

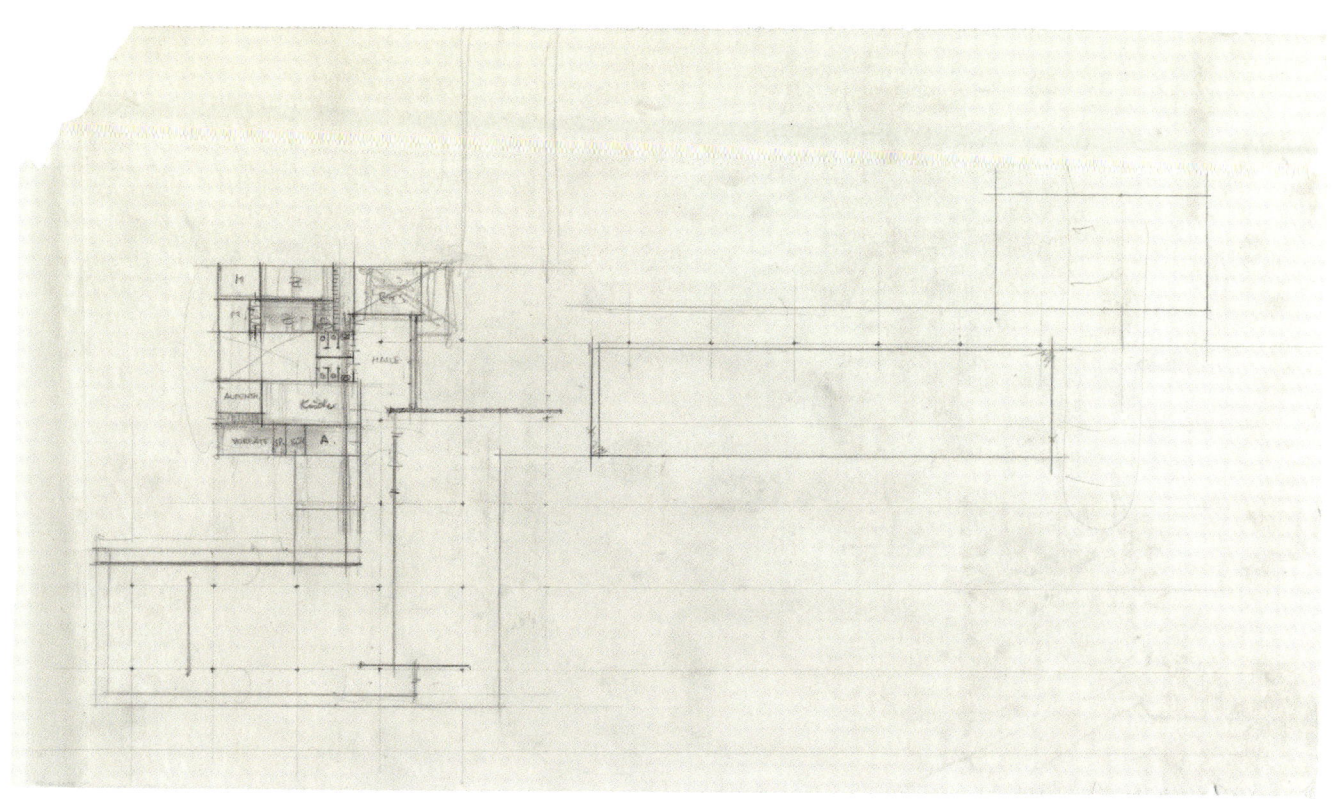

**Floorplan, 1930
Pencil on tracing paper,
12 1/2 x 21 1/4" (31.8 x 54 cm)
The Mies van der Rohe Archive,
gift of the architect**

Grundrisszeichnung, 1930
Bleistift auf Transparentpapier,
31,8 x 54 cm
The Mies van der Rohe Archive,
Geschenk des Architekten

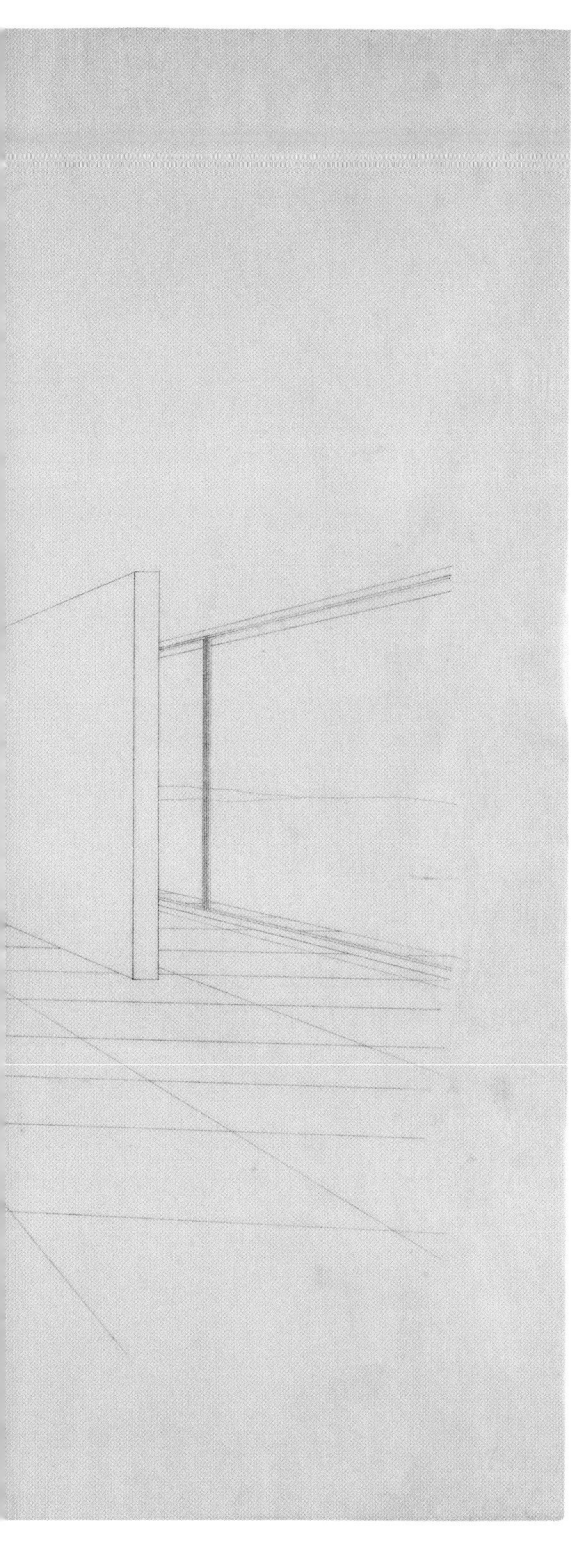

Interior perspective, 1930
Pencil on tracing paper,
28 1/4 x 39 1/2" (71.8 x 100.4 cm)
The Mies van der Rohe Archive,
gift of the architect

Perspektive, 1930
Bleistift auf Transparentpapier,
71,8 x 100,4 cm
The Mies van der Rohe Archive,
Geschenk des Architekten

**Interior perspective, 1930
Pencil on tracing paper,
28 1/2 x 39 1/2" (72.4 x 100.4 cm)
The Mies van der Rohe Archive,
gift of the architect**

Perspektive, 1930
Bleistift auf Transparentpapier,
72,4 x 100,4 cm
The Mies van der Rohe Archive,
Geschenk des Architekten

Perspective, 1930
Pencil on tracing paper,
28 1/2 x 39 1/2" (72.4 x 100.4 cm)
The Mies van der Rohe Archive,
gift of the architect

Perspektive, 1930
Bleistift auf Transparentpapier,
72,4 x 100,4 cm
The Mies van der Rohe Archive,
Geschenk des Architekten

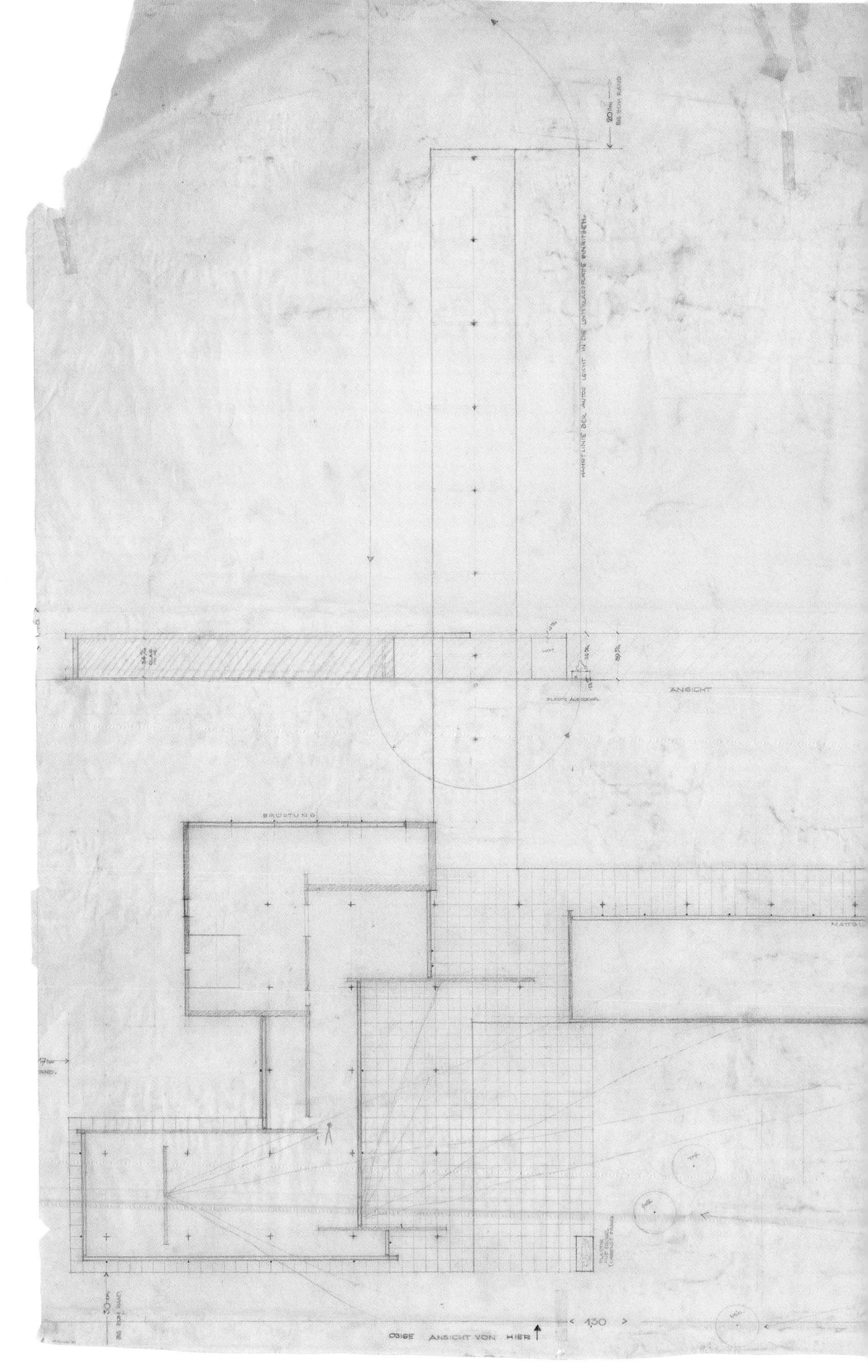

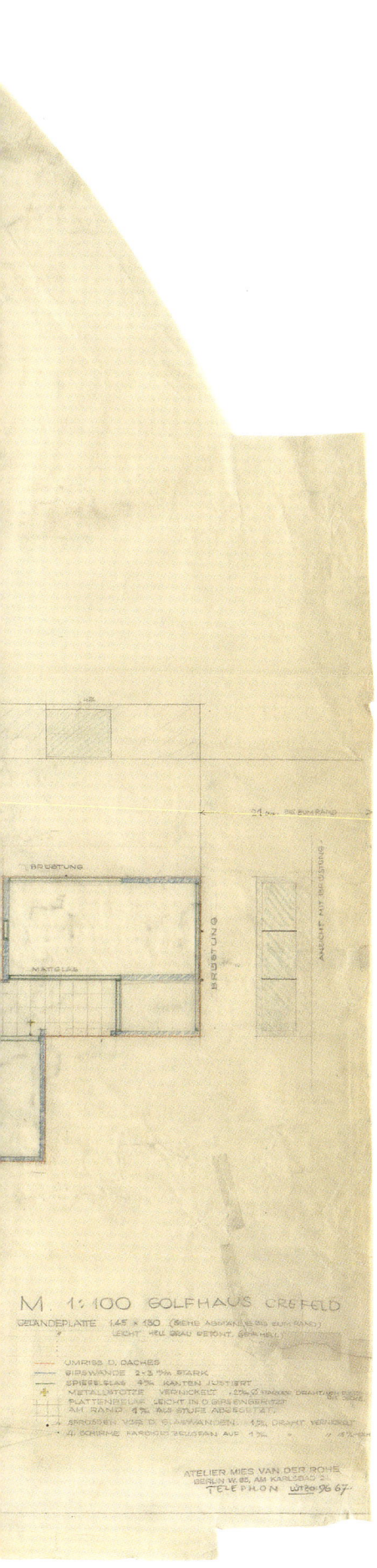

Floor plan and section, 1930
Pencil and colored pencil
on tracing paper,
44 1/2 x 41 3/4" (113 x 106 cm)
The Mies van der Rohe Archive,
gift of the architect

Grundriss und Schnitt, 1930
Bleistift und Kohle auf
Transparentpapier,
113 x 106 cm
The Mies van der Rohe Archive,
Geschenk des Architekten

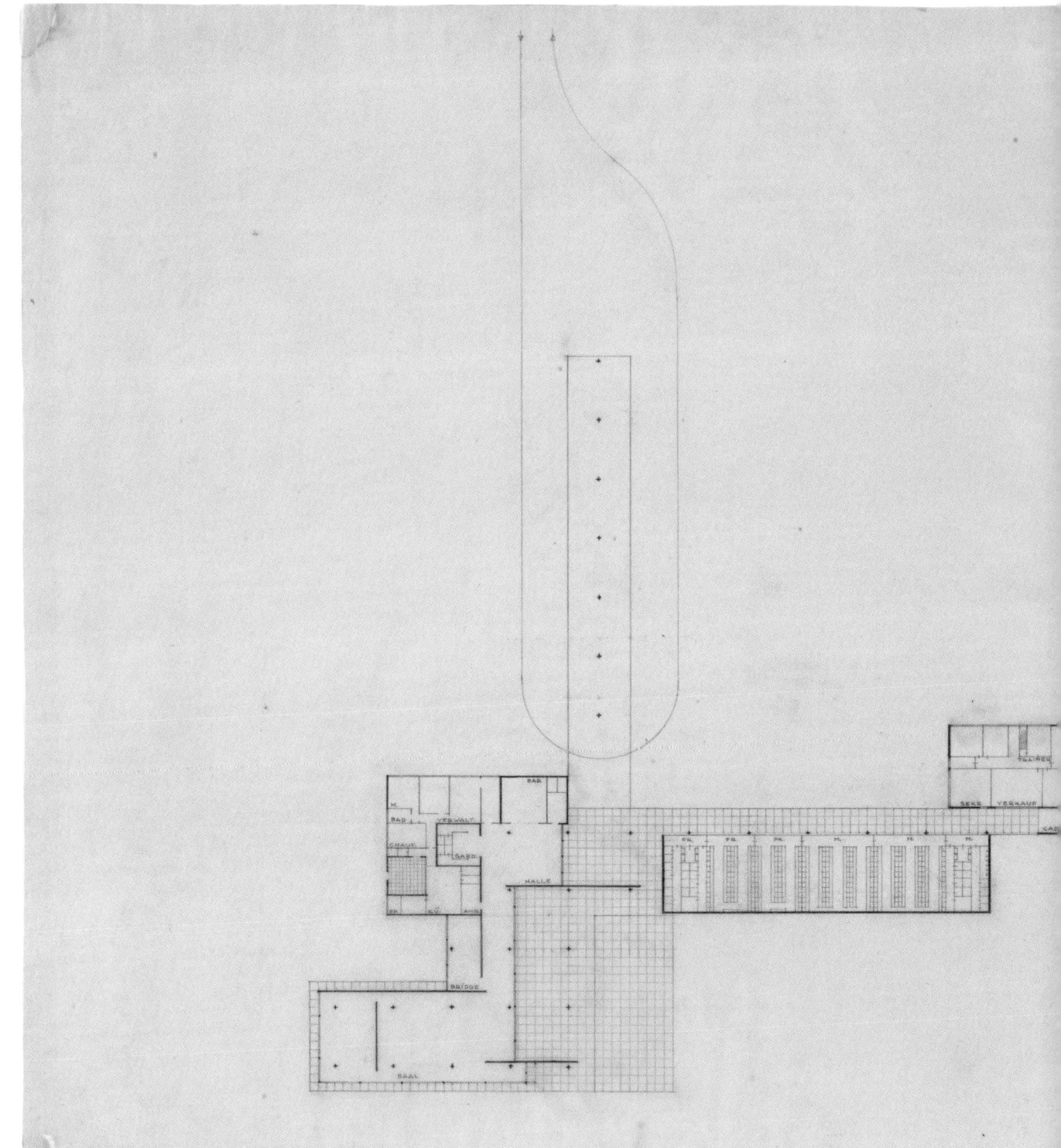

ENDGÜLTIGER ZUSTAND   MST 1:200

Floorplan, inscribed lower left:
„endgültiger Zustand"
(final version), 1930
Pencil on tracing paper,
27 x 31" (68.6 x 78.8 cm)
The Mies van der Rohe Archive,
gift of the architect

Grundriss, bezeichnet unten links:
„endgültiger Zustand", 1930
Bleistift auf Transparentpapier,
68,6 x 78,8 cm
The Mies van der Rohe Archive,
Geschenk des Architekten

MIES 1:1
The Golf club project

Christiane Lange

<u>An Architectural Model in the Landscape</u> *After a walk of about twenty minutes over trails and through meadows and wheat fields, the visitor sees an elegant building on the hilltop. Depending on the time of year, it appears from a distance as a flat, expansive, white building or simply as the line of a roof floating over swaying corn.*

Andreas Rossmann called the life-size architectural model of the Golf Club by Mies van der Rohe the "Fata Morgana of the architectural modernity." The model was constructed in the summer of 2013 on the hill named Egelsberg, close to the Rhine city of Krefeld.[1]

After its opening at the end of May 2013, the 1:1 model remained open day and night for five months. A constructed drawing, it allows Mies himself to speak silently about his architecture. Reminiscent of a memorial, it provides references to the historical context that provided the basis and "serves to remind" of the unusually long duration of Mies van der Rohe's cooperation with the Krefeld silk industry developers. Although temporary, it has opened "pathways to the past."[2] As an *objet d'architecture* by the Ghent-based architects Robbrecht en Daem, it escapes any clear definition.

1 Andreas Rossmann, "Fata Morgana der Architekturmoderne," in: *Frankfurter Allgemeine Zeitung*, Frankfurt am Main, No. 180, August 6, 2013, p. 28.
2 See text by Winfried Speitkamp, p. 170.

MIES 1:1
Das Golfclub Projekt

Christiane Lange

<u>Ein Architekturmodell in der Landschaft</u> Nach einem etwa 20-minütigem Fußmarsch über Feldwege durch Wiesen und Weizenfelder nähert sich der Besucher einem eleganten Bau auf der Kuppe des Hügels. Je nach Jahreszeit erblickt er aus der Ferne einen flachen, breitgelagerten weißen Gebäuderiegel oder lediglich eine schwebende Dachlinie über wogendem Getreide: „Fata Morgana der Architekturmoderne"[1] nennt Andreas Rossmann das lebensgroße Architekturmodell des Golfclubs von Mies van der Rohe, das im Sommer 2013 auf dem Egelsberg in der Nähe der rheinischen Stadt Krefeld errichtet war.

Nach seiner Eröffnung Ende Mai 2013 ist das 1:1-Modell fünf Monate lang Tag und Nacht zugänglich. Als gebaute Zeichnung lässt es Mies selbst wortlos über seine Architektur sprechen. Mit der Attitüde eines Denkmals verweist es auf den historischen Kontext, dem die zugrunde liegende Planung entsprungen ist und „erinnert" an die ungewöhnlich ausdauernde Zusammenarbeit Mies van der Rohes mit Krefelder Auftraggebern aus der Seidenindustrie. Obwohl temporär, öffnet es einen „Weg‚ in die Vergangenheit"[2]. Und als *objet d'architecture* der Genter Architekten Robbrecht en Daem entzieht es sich letztlich der eindeutigen Festlegung.

[1] Andreas Rossmann, „Fata Morgana der Architekturmoderne", in: *Frankfurter Allgemeine Zeitung*, Frankfurt a. M., Nr. 180, 6.8.2013, S. 28.
[2] Siehe Text von Winfried Speitkamp in diesem Band, S. 171.

Over a period of five months, it was used as a venue for art and a place for thought in which lectures, concerts, readings, a ballet evening or a poetry slam took place.³

Title plates with explanatory information were deliberately dispensed with. The 1:1 model is an exhibit, not an exhibition; however, well-informed Ciceroni were available at the site to provide visitors with information on the history and meaning of what they saw.

In 1930, Ludwig Mies van der Rohe designed an expansive clubhouse for Krefeld's first golf club. As was also the case in Berlin and Wuppertal, the founding initiative came from the wealthy citizens of the city. In Krefeld, these were mainly representatives of the local velvet and silk industry for whom Mies had already completed five projects in the period following 1927. Four more were to follow prior to his emigration to the USA in 1938. Mies van der Rohe's extensive work for developers in the Krefeld silk industry—numbering nine projects in total ⁴—laid the foundations in 2010 for an exhibition concept which then, in 2013, resulted in the temporary realization of the best design as a 1:1 model.

Mies 1:1 Golf Club Project is the title of this very special architectural exhibition. Paul Robbrecht, the Belgian architect, together with the associates of his practice, Robbrecht en Daem architecten, gave a well-conceptualized appearance to the design—which was already over eighty years old—for its temporary "performance" as a 1:1 model. It was not to be documents, plans, sketches, photographs, or drawings, but rather a single exhibit that was to provide the basis for the documentation of this unique series of contracts in Mies van der Rohe's oeuvre, together with their industrial and cultural context. The 1:1 model also serves to visualize Mies' architecture at the zenith of its European development.

Mies himself provided the impulse to this approach. One of the myths of his biography is the story of a design for the German-Dutch collector couple Helene Kröller-Müller and Anton Kröller. In 1911, the couple contacted several architects to provide designs for a residential house, which was also to house their extensive collection of modern art. Among them was Peter Behrens, one of the leading German architects of that time, in whose employment Mies happened to be. Behrens' suggestion, however, did not convince Helene Kröller-Müller. Mies, then twenty-five years old, was given the opportunity to present his design.⁵

It is not clear in detail how the story progressed from there. However, it is known that the couple had both designs constructed—the one from Behrens and the one from Mies—as 1:1 models, complete with roof battens and whitewashed canvas, at the planned site. A small number of photographs offer testimony of these models. They are impressive simply on the grounds of their sheer size. Their appearance is a little like stage scenery. For construction reasons, some parts appear to be a little roughly done. In the end, neither Behrens nor Mies succeeded in winning the contract. These models were also not used as a point of orientation for the Krefeld 1:1 model of 2013.

The remarkable thing about the story is the simple fact that these models ever actually existed. What might have prompted Anton Kröller,

3 See Chronology, pp. 204–207.
4 See: Christiane Lange, *Ludwig Mies van der Rohe, Architecture for the Silk Industry*, Berlin 2011.
5 Cf. Franz Schulze, *Mies van der Rohe. A Critical Biography*, Chicago, 1985, pp. 58–65.

Gelegentlich wird es zu einem Ort der Kunst und des Denkens, an dem Vorträge, Konzerte, Lesungen, ein Ballettabend oder ein Poetry-Slam stattfinden.[3]

Auf Texttafeln mit erläuternden Informationen wurde verzichtet. Das 1:1-Modell ist ein Exponat, keine Ausstellung. Es stehen jedoch täglich sachkundige Ciceroni zur Verfügung, die die Besucher über die Geschichte und Bedeutung dessen, was sie dort sehen, informieren.

1930 hatte Ludwig Mies van der Rohe für diesen Ort ein weitläufiges Clubhaus für Krefelds ersten Golfclub entworfen. Wie in Berlin oder Wuppertal ging auch hier die Initiative der Gründung von vermögenden Bürgern der Stadt aus. In Krefeld waren das vor allem Vertreter der ortsansässigen Samt- und Seidenindustrie, für die Mies seit 1927 bereits fünf Projekte realisiert hatte. Drei weitere sollten bis zu seiner Übersiedlung in die USA 1938 folgen. Diese umfangreiche Tätigkeit Mies van der Rohes für Auftraggeber der in Krefeld konzentrierten Seidenindustrie – insgesamt neun Projekte gingen aus ihr hervor[4] – bot 2010 den Ausgangspunkt einer Ausstellungsidee, die 2013 dann in der temporären Verwirklichung des besten Entwurfs als 1:1-Modell resultierte.

Mies 1:1 Das Golfclub Projekt lautet der Titel dieser besonderen Art von Architekturausstellung. Der belgische Architekt Paul Robbrecht und sein Büro Robbrecht en Daem architecten gaben dem über 80 Jahre alten Entwurf eine wohldurchdachte Erscheinung für seinen vorübergehenden irdischen Auftritt als 1:1-Modell. Nicht Dokumente, Pläne, Skizzen, Fotos und Zeichnungen sollten diese in der Biografie von Mies van der Rohe einmalige Auftragsserie und ihren industriell-kulturellen Kontext dokumentieren, sondern ein einzelnes Exponat. Zugleich vergegenwärtigt das 1:1-Modell Mies van der Rohes Architektur auf dem Höhepunkt ihrer europäischen Entwicklung.

Mies selbst gab den Anstoß zu diesem Ansatz. Zu den Mythen seiner Biografie gehört die Geschichte eines Entwurfs für das deutsch-niederländische Sammlerehepaar Helene Kröller-Müller und Anton Kröller. 1911 war das Paar mit mehreren Architekten in Kontakt getreten um diese um Entwürfe für ein Wohnhaus zu bitten, das gleichzeitig ihre umfangreiche Sammlung zeitgenössischer Kunst beherbergen sollte. Unter ihnen war Peter Behrens, einer der führenden deutschen Architekten jener Zeit, zu dessen Mitarbeitern Mies damals zählte. Behrens Vorschlag konnte Helene Kröller-Müller jedoch nicht überzeugen und so erhielt der gerade 25-jährige Mies die Möglichkeit, seinen Entwurf vorzulegen.[5]

Die genauen Umstände der weiteren Geschichte sind nicht im Detail überliefert. Belegt ist, dass das Ehepaar beide Entwürfe – sowohl den von Behrens als auch den von Mies – als Modell aus Dachlatten und geweißter Leinwand im Maßstab 1:1 am geplanten Bauplatz errichten ließ. Die durch ihre schiere Größe beeindruckenden Modelle sind auf wenigen Fotografien überliefert. Sie hatten eine kulissenhafte Erscheinung, die Ausführung war in einigen Teilen wohl aus konstruktiven Gründen etwas grob ausgefallen. Den erhofften Auftrag brachten sie jedoch weder Behrens noch Mies. Und auch dem Krefelder 1:1-Modell von 2013 dienten sie nicht als Orientierung.

Bemerkenswert an dieser Geschichte ist vielmehr die Tatsache, *dass* es diese Modelle überhaupt gegeben hat. Was mag wohl den erfolgreichen

[3] Siehe Chronik der Veranstaltungen in diesem Band, S. 204–207.
[4] Vgl. Christiane Lange, *Ludwig Mies van der Rohe. Architektur für die Seidenindustrie*, Berlin 2011.
[5] Vgl. Franz Schulze, *Mies van der Rohe. Leben und Werk*, Berlin 1986, S. 65–73.

a successful entrepreneur, to go to such lengths in spite of the obvious challenges involved in the logistics of such an undertaking? Was he mistrustful of the images of the planned architecture? Did he believe that architecture could only be truly comprehended in its three-dimensional manifestation? What kind of impressions might these canvas models have left on Mies? Rem Koolhaas has questions on this: "Were its whiteness and weightlessness an overwhelming revelation of everything he did not yet believe in?" Was it, perhaps, the beginning of his "tectonics of disappearance, dissolution, floating?" [6] Koolhaas, like the Kröller-Müllers, although observing from a contrary perspective, could see the ambiguous quality of a full-scale model as a physically experiential architectural concept.

The Krefeld Textile Industry and the Golf Club Competition of 1930

"A flat, expansive, white cone presiding over its surroundings and offering a view sweeping from the south to the west to the north, encompassing the whole of that wide-open landscape." [7]

Ludwig Mies van der Rohe used these words in 1930 to describe the location of the planned clubhouse. In the summer of 1930, one of the leading architectural practices in the golf scene, "Vereinigte Golfarchitekten" (united golf architects), had already been issued the contract for the golf course.[8] Besides Mies van der Rohe, the club had also approached August Biebricher for a design. Biebricher was a representative of a subdued modernity and locally a very successful architect.

The division of space demanded was sent to both architects in August 1930, together with the competition documents. The sports utilities were to include changing rooms for 250 people, a trainers' area with apartment, workshop, saleroom, and caddy room. The housekeepers' area was to consist of kitchen, service area, wine cellar and storeroom, as well as an apartment for the housekeeper. For the society-and-events component of the complex, the potential customer wanted a large hall with a separate bridge room, as well as a terrace with an "open air dance floor." [9] The location and the access to the clubhouse had already been fixed and laid down. Krefelder Golf Club e.V. had calculated building costs of around 150,000 reichsmarks. A further 30,000 reichsmarks were available for the implementation of the interior design.

Although Mies was very busy in the summer of 1930, he confirmed by return post that he would make a contribution to the competition within six weeks. The task would probably have aroused his appetite. It offered him the possibility of realizing a prestigious project within a trusted circle of customers. The expansive clubhouse, to be designed for around 250 players, was to become a meeting place with interregional attraction. Aside from that, the topographical situation was unusual: the undeveloped landscape offered a creative scope previously unknown to Mies, allowing him to combine his architecture and the surrounding nature with a greatly increased degree of freedom.

At this point in time, Mies was already a celebrated architect. Ever since the success of the German Pavilion at the 1929 World Exhibition in Barcelona, his fame had spread as far as New York. He was in the process of

6 "Were its whiteness and weightlessness an overwelming revelation of everything he did not yet believe in? ... tectonics of disappearance, dissolution, floating ... " Rem Koolhaas, "The house that Made Mies", in: O.M.A., Rem Koolhaas, Bruce Mau, *S,M,L,XL*, Rotterdam, 1995, p. 63.
7 Ludwig Mies van der Rohe, commentary to "Projekt einer Klubhausanlage für den Krefelder Golf-Klub e.V." 1930, Late German Projects, The Museum of Modern Art. The Mies van der Rohe Archive, New York.
8 "Vereinigte Golfarchitekten", F. G. Fahrenholtz, Karl Hoffmann, and Charles A. Mackenzie.
9 Krefelder Golf Club e.V., Bau eines Clubhauses mit Nebenräumen für den Krefelder Golf-Club e.V., 1930, Late German Projects, The Museum of Modern Art. The Mies van der Rohe Archive, New York.

Unternehmer Anton Kröller dazu veranlasst haben, diesen Aufwand jenseits aller Verwertungslogik zu betreiben? Traute er den Bildern der geplanten Architektur nicht? War er der Ansicht, dass Architektur nur in ihrer dreidimensionalen Materialisierung wirklich erfasst werden könne?

Und welchen Eindruck hat das Leinwandmodell wohl bei Mies selbst hinterlassen? So fragt sich Rem Koolhaas: „Offenbarte es mit seiner Helligkeit und Leichtigkeit in überwältigender Weise all das, was er noch nicht glauben konnte?" War es der Anfang seiner „Tektonik des Verschwindens, der Auflösung und des Fließens?"[6] Koolhaas wie auch das Ehepaar Kröller-Müller erkannten aus gegensätzlichen Blickrichtungen die ambivalente Qualität des lebensgroßen Modells als physisch erfahrbares architektonisches Konzept.

Die Krefelder Textilindustrie und der Golfclub-Wettbewerb von 1930

„Breitgelagerter, kahler Kegel, der die Landschaft weithin beherrscht und von dem von Süden über Westen nach Norden der Blick über die weite Landschaft schweift."[7]

Mit diesen Worten beschrieb Ludwig Mies van der Rohe 1930 den Standort des zu planenden Clubhauses. Mit der Anlage des Golfplatzes war im Sommer 1930 bereits eines der führenden Büros der Golfszene, die „Vereinigten Golfarchitekten" beauftragt worden.[8] Für den Entwurf des Clubhauses hatte der Verein neben Mies van der Rohe auch den lokal sehr erfolgreichen Architekten August Biebricher, Vertreter einer gemäßigten Moderne, um einen Entwurf gebeten.

In den Ausschreibungsunterlagen, die beide Architekten im August 1930 erhielten, war das geforderte Raumprogramm beschrieben. Für den sportlichen Teil sollte eine Umkleide für 250 Personen und ein Trainerbereich mit Wohnung, Werkstatt, Verkaufs- und Caddyraum geschaffen werden. Der Wirtschaftsbereich umfasste Küche, Anrichte, Weinkeller und Vorratsräume sowie eine Wirtschafterwohnung. Für den gesellschaftlichen Teil der Anlage wünschten die potenziellen Auftraggeber schließlich einen großen Saal mit separatem Bridgeraum sowie eine Terrasse „mit Tanzplatz im Freien"[9]. Standort und Zufahrt des zu planenden Clubgebäudes waren vorgegeben. Der Verein hatte Baukosten in Höhe von 150 000 Reichsmark veranschlagt. Weitere 30 000 Reichsmark standen für die Innenausstattung zur Verfügung.

Obwohl Mies im Sommer 1930 sehr beschäftigt war, sagte er postwendend zu, innerhalb von sechs Wochen einen Wettbewerbsbeitrag zu erarbeiten. Die Aufgabe wird ihn gereizt haben. Sie bot ihm die Gelegenheit, für einen wohlvertrauten Kundenkreis ein Prestigeprojekt zu verwirklichen. Das weitläufige Clubhaus für etwa 250 Spieler würde ein gesellschaftlicher Treffpunkt mit überregionaler Strahlkraft werden. Außerdem war die topografische Situation außergewöhnlich: Die unbebaute Landschaft ermöglichte Mies in einer bis dahin unübertroffenen Freiheit seine Architektur mit der umgebenden Natur zu verbinden.

Mies war zu diesem Zeitpunkt bereits ein gefeierter Architekt. Seit dem Erfolg des Repräsentationspavillons des Deutschen Reiches auf der Weltausstellung in Barcelona 1929 war sein Ruf bis nach New York vorgedrungen. Er konzipierte gerade die Ausstellung *Die Wohnung unserer*

---

[6] „Were its whiteness and weightlessness an overwelming revelation of everything he did not yet believe in? ... tectonics of disappearance, dissolution, floating ..." Rem Koolhaas, „The house that made Mies", in: O.M.A., Rem Koolhaas, Bruce Mau, *S, M, L, XL*, Rotterdam 1995, S. 63.
[7] Ludwig Mies van der Rohe, Kommentar zum „Projekt einer Klubhausanlage für den Krefelder Golf-Klub e.V.", 1930, Late German Projects, The Museum of Modern Art. The Mies van der Rohe Archive, New York.
[8] „Vereinigte Golfarchitekten": F. G. Fahrenholtz, Karl Hoffmann und Charles A. Mackenzie.
[9] Krefelder Golf Club e.V., Bau eines Clubhauses mit Nebenräumen für den Krefelder Golf-Club e.V. 1930, Late German Projects, The Museum of Modern Art. The Mies van der Rohe Archive, New York.

creating a concept for the exhibition, *Die Wohnung unserer Zeit* (The Dwelling of Our Time), which was to take place within the scope of the 1931 Berlin Building Exhibition; he had taken up his position as Director of Bauhaus in Dessau; Haus Tugendhat in Brünn was nearing its completion; he was working, together with his partner Lilly Reich, on several interior designs for apartments, and he was extending his furniture repertoire. Lilly Reich represented him in his office and at the building exhibition while he was in Dessau. Without her organizational and communicative talents, it would not have been possible for him to take on all of these tasks.

At the beginning of the year, Mies had completed the planning and implementation of private villas in Krefeld for the textile factory owners Josef Esters and Hermann Lange, for which the invoicing process was still ongoing (Haus Lange, Haus Esters, 1927–1930, which today make up the Kunstmuseen Krefeld (Krefeld Art Museums)). He had also, along with Lilly Reich, just completed two sensational pieces of architecture for exhibitions for the Krefeld-based Verein Deutscher Seidenwebereien (Association of German Silk Weaving Mills). These were the *Velvet and Silk Cafe* for the 1927 Berlin "Fashion for Women" trade fair and the *German Silk* representation pavilion at the 1929 Barcelona World Exhibition.[10] Mies was also working with Lilly Reich on the interior design of an apartment for Mildred Crous, one of Hermann Lange's daughters (Crous Apartment, 1930). Following this, in the winter of 1930, also in Krefeld, came the dye works and men's lining materials building of the Vereinigte Seidenwebereien AG (United Silk Weaving Mills, abbreviated as Verseidag). This project was completed in 1931 and extended in 1935. Verseidag, based in Krefeld, was an association of several local silk factories founded under the leadership of Josef Esters and Hermann Lange in 1919. Since then it had developed to become one of the leading enterprises in the German silk industry. The building remained Mies' only factory building.

A further residential house planned in 1935 for Ulrich Lange, a son of Hermann Lange, as well as the planning of the Verseidag headquarters in 1937, served to extend the series of Krefeld contracts by one courtyard house and one administration building. Yet neither project could be built. The private residential house was not carried out due to the National Socialist building regulations, while the administration building was canceled shortly before the beginning of the war, possibly as a result of material shortage.

The unusual duration and diversity of Mies' cooperation with one and the same group of developers remained unique in his résumé. He and Lilly Reich referred to the group around the silk factory owner and collector Hermann Lange (mentioned in earlier research as the central figure and driving force in the relationship) as the "Krefelder Freunde" (Krefeld friends).

Study of the files of the Association of German Silk Weaving Mills, as well as those of the Deutscher Werkbund (founded in 1907), reveals a slightly different impression. In fact it was not just one individual who had prepared the grounds for this successful cooperation. In 1927, as Mies received his first Krefeld contract from the association, the rich silk city already had a history of industrial design stretching back three

10 The following is based on: Christiane Lange, *Ludwig Mies van der Rohe. Architecture for the Silk Industry*, Berlin 2011.

Zeit, die im Rahmen der Bauausstellung in Berlin 1931 stattfinden sollte und hatte seine Tätigkeit als Direktor des Bauhauses in Dessau angetreten. Haus Tugendhat in Brünn stand kurz vor der Fertigstellung. Gemeinsam mit seiner Partnerin Lilly Reich arbeitete er an mehreren Wohnungseinrichtungen und erweiterte sein Möbelrepertoire. Ohne das organisatorische und kommunikative Talent von Lilly Reich, die ihn in seinem Büro und bei der Bauausstellung vertrat, während er selbst in Dessau war, wäre es ihm sicherlich nicht möglich gewesen, alle diese Aufgaben zu bewältigen.

In Krefeld hatte Mies Anfang des Jahres die Planung und Ausführung der privaten Wohnhäuser für die Textilfabrikanten Josef Esters und Hermann Lange abgeschlossen (Haus Lange, Haus Esters, 1927–1930, heute Kunstmuseen Krefeld) – die Abrechnung war noch im Gange – und gemeinsam mit Lilly Reich zwei aufsehenerregende Ausstellungsarchitekturen für den in Krefeld ansässigen Branchenverband der Seidenindustrie „Verein Deutscher Seidenwebereien" realisiert: Das *Café Samt & Seide* für die Messe *Die Mode der Dame* in Berlin 1927 und den Repräsentationspavillon *Deutsche Seide* auf der Weltausstellung in Barcelona 1929.[10] Ebenfalls mit Lilly Reich arbeitete Mies an einer Wohnungseinrichtung für Mildred Crous, eine der Töchter von Hermann Lange (Wohnung Crous, 1930). Im Winter 1930 sollte das Färberei- und HE-Gebäude der Vereinigten Seidenwebereien AG (kurz: Verseidag) in Krefeld folgen, das 1931 verwirklicht und 1935 erweitert wurde. Die in Krefeld ansässige Verseidag war eine Vereinigung mehrerer ortsansässiger Seidenfabriken, die unter der Leitung von Josef Esters und Hermann Lange 1919 gegründet worden war und sich zum führenden Unternehmen der deutschen Seidenindustrie entwickelt hatte. Das Gebäude blieb Mies' einziger Fabrikbau.

10 Die folgende Darstellung basiert auf: Christiane Lange, *Ludwig Mies van der Rohe. Architektur für die Seidenindustrie*, Berlin 2011.

Ein weiteres Wohnhaus für Ulrich Lange, ein Sohn Hermann Langes, 1935 und die Planung der Hauptverwaltung der Verseidag 1937 erweiterten die Auftragsserie aus Krefeld um ein Hofhaus und einen Verwaltungsbau. Beide Projekte konnten nicht mehr gebaut werden. Das private Wohnhaus fiel der nationalsozialistischen Baugestaltungsordnung zum Opfer, der Verwaltungsbau kurz vor Kriegsbeginn vermutlich der Materialknappheit.

In Mies' Biografie blieb die ungewöhnliche Ausdauer und Vielfalt der Zusammenarbeit mit ein und derselben Auftraggebergruppe eine Ausnahme. „Krefelder Freunde" nannten er und Lilly Reich den Kreis um den Seidenfabrikanten und Sammler Hermann Lange, den die ältere Forschung als zentrale Figur und Motor der Verbindung ansah.

Die Durchsicht der Akten des Vereins deutscher Seidenwebereien sowie des Deutschen Werkbundes konnte dieses Bild differenzieren. Nicht eine einzelne Person hatte das Feld bereitet, auf dem sich diese Zusammenarbeit so erfolgreich entwickeln konnte. 1927, als Mies vom Branchenverband der Seidenindustrie seinen ersten Auftrag aus Krefeld erhalten hatte, blickte die reiche Seidenstadt bereits auf eine fast drei Jahrzehnte andauernde Auseinandersetzung mit industrieller Gestaltung zurück. Das örtliche Kunstgewerbemuseum unter der Leitung eines führenden Vertreters des Deutschen Werkbundes, Friedrich Deneken, hatte schon um 1900 damit begonnen, in Krefeld Handwerk und Industrie

decades. The local Applied Arts Museum, which was under the leadership of Friedrich Deneken, a leading representative of the Deutscher Werkbund, had already, in 1900, begun to bring tradesmen and industry in Krefeld in contact with artists of the reform movement, creating an emphasis on "refinement of taste" (for example, Peter Behrens, Otto Eckmann, and Henry van de Velde). It was the beginning of a cooperation that, over the next decades, was to lead to the forging of many relationships between the silk industry, the Deutscher Werkbund, and representatives of the avant-garde of design such as László Moholy-Nagy and Johannes Itten, as well as other teachers and students of Bauhaus. This network became a tool that the Association of German Silk Weaving Mills utilized in the mid-1920s when it recognized the need for public relations work as a result of growing international competition. The *Velvet and Silk Cafe* was the first initiative on the part of the German silk industry to cultivate a public image. The German Silk Pavilion for Barcelona World Exhibition was the first international appearance. The connection to the artistic avant-garde achieved the declared goal of modernizing the face of German satin and silk production.

The series of Krefeld commissions can therefore be said to have come about within the context of a dynamic cooperation of economic-communicative interests between the German silk industry and the Deutscher Werkbund, as well as being a result of artistic and innovative entrepreneurship that was active throughout Europe. In the case of the Golf Club Project, economic interests could well have been unified with societal interests. The competition, however, was closed undecided. The financial means could no longer be made available due to the economic crisis. In 1931, the Krefeld Golf Club e.V. moved into an empty villa close to the completed golf course. Mies received a participant's fee of five hundred reichsmarks and the project was declared closed.

11 See Note 7.
12 Ludwig Mies van der Rohe, 1930, Late German Projects, The Museum of Modern Art. The Mies van der Rohe Archive, New York.

<u>The Golf Club Design by Mies</u> "The wide cone of land needs a flat, expansive building that will blend in with the landscape. The view demands that the building should be open to the south, the west and the north."[11]

In Mies van der Rohe's estate in the Museum of Modern Art in New York, there are around eighty drawings, sketches, and plans for the Golf Club Competition.[12] A solution verging on the utopian, with parts of the building underground in the hill, was rejected for an expansive flat building, parts of which jut out eccentrically into the landscape. In accordance with the points of the compass, it lay cross-shaped on the summit of the hill.

Robbrecht en Daem architecten had several sketches, plans, and perspectives at their disposal for the reconstruction of Mies' design idea: A section through the building and a layout plan labeled with the words "endgültiger Zustand" (final state) offer detailed information on the entire design, as well as on how Mies had intended to allocate the functional areas [ill. p. 62–63]. The rooms are clearly labeled "hall," "lobby," "changing rooms," "terrace," "bridge room," etc. Views of the individual façades and illustrated drawings were not available and it is difficult to know whether they ever existed. Instead, there are several perspectives to be found in the estate. These show the access road with the entrance

im Sinne der „Geschmacksveredlung" in Kontakt mit Künstlern der Reformbewegung wie Peter Behrens, Otto Eckmann oder Henry van de Velde zu bringen. Es war der Auftakt einer Auseinandersetzung, die in den nächsten Jahrzehnten zu vielfältigen Verbindungen der Seidenindustrie mit dem 1907 gegründete Deutschen Werkbund und Vertretern der gestalterischen Avantgarde führen sollte, wie zum Beispiel mit László Moholy-Nagy und Johannes Itten sowie weiteren Lehrern und Schülern des Bauhauses. Als der Verband der Seidenindustrie Mitte der 1920er-Jahre erkannte, dass es aufgrund der wachsenden internationalen Konkurrenz notwendig geworden war, Öffentlichkeitsarbeit zu betreiben, griff er auf dieses Netzwerk zurück. Das *Café Samt & Seide* war die erste öffentliche Selbstdarstellung der deutschen Seidenindustrie auf nationaler Ebene, der Pavillon *Deutsche Seide* stellte den ersten internationalen Auftritt dar. Die Verbindung mit der künstlerischen Avantgarde erreichte das erklärte Ziel, das Image der deutschen Samt- und Seidenproduktion zu modernisieren.

Die Krefelder Auftragsserie entstand somit im Kontext eines dynamischen Zusammenspiels der ökonomisch-kommunikativen Interessen der deutschen Seidenindustrie mit dem Deutschen Werkbund, getragen von einem kunstsinnigen, innovationsfreudigen Unternehmertum, das europaweit agierte. Im Golfclub Projekt hätten sich die ökonomischen mit den gesellschaftlichen Interessen vereinen können. Der Wettbewerb wurde jedoch nie entschieden, da die finanziellen Mittel aufgrund der Wirtschaftskrise nicht mehr aufzubringen waren. Der Verein bezog 1931 eine leerstehende Villa in der Nähe des fertiggestellten Platzes. Mit dem Erhalt des Teilnehmerhonorars von 500 Reichsmark war das Projekt für Mies beendet.

Der Golfclub-Entwurf von Mies   „Der breite Geländekegel verlangt eine sich in die Landschaft einschmiegende, breitgelagerte, flache Anlage. Die Aussicht verlangt eine sich nach Süden, Westen, Norden öffnende Anlage."[11]

Im Nachlass Mies van der Rohes im Museum of Modern Art in New York befinden sich circa 80 Zeichnungen, Skizzen und Pläne zum Golfclub-Wettbewerb.[12] Eine fast utopisch anmutende Lösung mit unterirdisch in den Hügel hineinreichenden Gebäudeteilen wurde verworfen zugunsten einer weitläufigen Anlage, deren Gebäudeteil exzentrisch in die Landschaft auskragt. Den Himmelsrichtungen folgend lag sie wie ein Kreuz auf der Hügelkuppe.

Für die Rekonstruktion der Mies'schen Entwurfsidee standen Robbrecht en Daem architecten mehrere Skizzen, Pläne und Perspektiven zur Verfügung: Ein Schnitt durch das Gebäude und ein Grundriss mit der Beschriftung „endgültiger Zustand" geben detailliert Auskunft darüber, wie Mies die Gesamtanlage und die Verteilung der Funktionsbereiche geplant hatte [Abb. S. 62–63]. Die Räume sind als „Halle", „Saal", „Umkleide", „Terrasse", „Bridgeraum" etc. eindeutig benannt. Aufrisse der einzelnen Fassaden und illustrierende Zeichnungen sind jedoch nicht überliefert und es ist fraglich, ob sie jemals existiert haben. Stattdessen befinden sich mehrere Perspektiven im Nachlass. Sie zeigen die Zufahrt mit Eingangsbereich [Abb. S. 48–49] und die Terrasse sowie mehrere

11 Siehe Anm. 7.
12 Ludwig Mies van der Rohe, 1930, Late German Projects, The Museum of Modern Art. The Mies van der Rohe Archive, New York.

area [ill. p. 48–49] and the terrace, as well as several views of the "hall" and the "lobby" in the societal-and-events area [ill. pp. 54–57]. Mies' attention was not, however, on the details of the design. The question of the materials that would be used as well as other details had not yet been addressed. Mies' interest was far more focused on the views through the building, and on the building within the landscape. With these perspectives, he illustrates using just a few fine lines—which was typical for him—his idea of space and of the interweaving of architecture with the surrounding nature.

Mies has developed the functional areas demanded in the competition documents as separate structures brought together under a single roof. The arrangement of the building structures has been carefully developed in small sketches [ill. p. 52–53]. The grid of the supporting structure, which he drew in at the beginning with light strokes, serves as a starting point and as the basis of the composition. In the sketch it has the function of the bass-line, the bars of which can be said to be the visible *meter*, while freestanding walls and window elements are set in syncopated relationship to these elements. Mies' deep conviction that the "construction" provides the basis of architecture is clearly visible here: "The structure is the backbone of the whole and makes the variable floor plan possible. Without this backbone, the floor plan could not be free but would be chaotically blocked."[13]

The grounds of the club were to be accessible via an access road in the east. A fifty-meter-long canopy, supported by seven centrally positioned pillars, leads the visitor to the entrance while offering protection from sun and rain. Mies gave a great deal of attention to the access road. He added the driving lane of the vehicles decoratively to the floor plan and, in one of the few color perspectives, he drew a stylish sports car in front of the entrance. Due to the fact that the location is in the outskirts of the city, he justifies his "consideration of the prospective traffic"[14] matter-of-factly [ill. pp. 47, 48–49].

The changing rooms and trainers' area provide a complementary piece to the access road, stretching out in a long tract towards the south. Mies emphasizes that the sports area must be separate from the societal-and-events area of the complex. In consideration of this, the changing room opens solely onto the access-road side with a glass façade behind a row of supports. On the terrace side it is closed hermetically, in order to make it possible for golfers to go straight from the golf course to the changing rooms without having to go through the societal-and-events part of the complex.

The societal focus of the clubhouse is the "Hall." Mies' concept included it on the west side of the building, similar to a belvedere. If the observer looks out of this room, which is completely made of glass on three sides, from a slightly elevated position, a remarkable view of the surrounding nature is revealed. Typically for Mies' work, freestanding walls at the north and west sides present the panorama in framed views. Mies depicted the view of the surrounding landscape in several perspectives, employing the grid of the floor tiles as perspective construction lines [ill. pp. 55–58]. They attract the eye to the vanishing point where the

13 Christian Norberg-Schulz, "Ein Gespräch mit Mies van der Rohe" (A Conversation with Mies van der Rohe), in: *Baukunst und Werkform*, Year 11, Magazine 11, 1958, p. 615.
14 Ludwig Mies van der Rohe, commentary on the competition design, see Note 7.

Ansichten der „Halle" und des „Saals" im gesellschaftlichen Bereich [Abb. S. 54–57]. Hier galt Mies' Aufmerksamkeit jedoch nicht den Gestaltungsdetails. Die Frage der zu verwendenden Materialien wie auch vieler anderer Details war noch nicht beantwortet. Sein Interesse galt den Ausblicken durch das Gebäude und vom Gebäude in die Landschaft. Mit diesen Perspektiven veranschaulichte Mies in der für ihn typischen Weise mit wenigen feinen Linien seine Idee von Raum und von der Verzahnung der Architektur mit der umgebenden Natur.

Die in der Ausschreibung geforderten Funktionsbereiche bildet Mies als getrennte Volumen aus und fasst sie unter einer Dachfläche zusammen. Die Anordnung der Baukörper entwickelte er sorgfältig in kleinen Skizzen [Abb. S. 52, 53]. Das Raster des Tragwerks, das er zu Beginn mit leichten Strichen auf das Blatt zeichnet, dient ihm hierbei als Ausgangspunkt und Grundlage der Komposition. Im Entwurf hat es die Funktion der Basslinie, deren Taktpunkte die sichtbaren Stützen bilden, Wandscheiben und Fensterelemente sind dazu in ein synkopisches Verhältnis gesetzt. Mies' tiefe Überzeugung von der „Konstruktion" als Grundlage der Architektur wird hier deutlich: „Die Struktur ist das Rückgrat des Ganzen und macht den variablen Grundriss möglich. Ohne dieses Rückgrat wäre der Grundriss nicht frei sondern chaotisch blockiert."[13]

Das Clubgelände sollte über eine Zufahrt im Osten erschlossen werden. Ein 50 Meter langes Vordach, getragen von sieben Mittelstützen, leitet den Ankommenden zum Eingang und bietet Schutz vor Sonne und Regen. Der Zufahrt schenkt Mies große Aufmerksamkeit. Er fügt die Spur der Fahrzeuge wie ein Ornament in den Grundriss ein und zeigt in einer der wenigen farbigen Perspektiven einen schicken Sportwagen vor dem Eingang. Mit der Lage am Stadtrand begründet er seine „Rücksichtnahme auf den voraussichtlichen Autoverkehr"[14] sachlich [Abb. S. 47, 48–49].

Als Pendant zur Zufahrt erstreckt sich die Umkleide mit Trainerbereich als langer Trakt weit nach Süden. Mies betont, dass der sportliche Bereich vom gesellschaftlichen zu trennen sei. Entsprechend öffnet sich die Umkleide nur auf der Seite der Zufahrt mit einer Glasfassade hinter einer Stützenreihe, während sie auf der Terrassenseite hermetisch verschlossen bleibt. Der Golfer sollte sie nach dem Spiel vom Platz aus erreichen können, ohne den gesellschaftlichen Teil durchqueren zu müssen.

Den gesellschaftlichen Mittelpunkt des Clubhauses bildet der „Saal". Mies konzipiert ihn auf der Westseite der Anlage ähnlich einem Belvedere. Aus leicht erhöhter Position bietet der auf drei Seiten vollständig verglaste Raum einen außergewöhnlichen Ausblick in die umgebende Natur. Frei stehende Wandscheiben auf der Nord- und auf der Westseite gliedern das Panorama in der für Mies typischen Weise in gerahmte Ausblicke. In mehreren Perspektiven stellt er den Blick vom Innenraum in die umgebende Landschaft dar [Abb. S. 54–57]. Das Raster der Bodenplatten nutzt er hierbei wie perspektivische Konstruktionslinien. Sie ziehen den Blick zum Fluchtpunkt, wo der „gewellte Horizont gegen die perfekte Horizontale"[15] läuft. Dass sich diese Darstellung im Widerspruch zum Grundriss befindet, der gar keinen gerasterten Boden im Innenbereich vorsieht, stört Mies nicht. Es geht ihm nicht darum, seinen Entwurf zu illustrieren, sondern um seine Idee von Raum.

13 Christian Norberg-Schulz, „Ein Gespräch mit Mies van der Rohe", in: *Baukunst und Werkform*, Jg. 11, Heft 11, 1958, S. 615.
14 Ludwig Mies van der Rohe, Kommentar zum Wettbewerbsentwurf, siehe Anm. 7.
15 Alexander Schwarz im Gespräch mit der Autorin am 12.5.2014, siehe in diesem Band S. 195.

"undulating horizon" approaches the "perfect horizontal."[15] The fact that this portrayal contradicts the floor plan, which does not include such a grid on the floor in the inside area, does not seem to bother Mies. The important thing for him is not to illustrate his design, but to unfold his notion of space.

In contrast to the open, spacious hall, Mies gives the bridge room a solitary character in accordance with its purpose. The adjacent lobby, which provides the architectural centerpiece of the building, is simultaneously the point at which all paths cross. The cloakroom is here, as are the entrances to the inn area, a small bar, and the telephone room.

Paul Robbrecht describes Mies' Golf Club design as a "missing masterpiece." Created at the culminating point of Mies' European career, it is witness to his mature architectural language, which he handles sovereignly. It belongs to a series of just a few designs which were carried out between 1928 and 1931 that rendered Mies' reputation no less than iconic: the Barcelona Pavilion of 1929; Haus Tugendhat in Brünn, 1928–31 and the specimen house at the 1931 Berlin Building Exhibition.

The 1:1 Model by Robbrecht en Daem architecten

Just as Mies formulated his idea of space clearly with a few well-placed lines, Robbrecht en Daem architecten translated this idea with the same degree of precision in minimalist forms and material language to an ephemeral *objet d'architecture* of the present. Similarly to Mies, for them the central consideration is not the exterior appearance of his planned architecture, but his architectural concept. They describe the process of approaching and implementing it as a development "from the impossible replica to a life-size model of Mies' design."[16] It is not empathy and speculation that mark their method of dealing with the available sources, but constructive distance. Mies would probably have referred to such an attitude as "service" rather than "self revelation."[17] The point of departure for the architects was not the prospect of completing Mies' design, extrapolating "in his spirit" the missing information from other projects in order to provide a more detailed picture. The point of orientation for the decisions involving the transposition of Mies' design to a 1:1 model was rather the architectural idea: whether and how, which materials, and to what extent Mies' instructions should be formulated in the sense of an architectural model rather than that of a functioning building.

The implementation of Mies' design to a 1:1 model opened a space between architectural idea and architectural construction: a space in which the freedom of the drawing could fuse with the strength of the physical presence. Only within this space was it possible to achieve a state of suspension between the abstract and the physical as possible experiences. The 1:1 model suspends a moment of transition on the way to completion—as in the raw shell or the disintegration to a ruin—in which "the naked architectural beauty is revealed."[18] "It depends on how long you remain suspended," said Thomas Schütte, referring to the fragile process of the transition from a conceptualized piece of architecture to a constructed one. With this he was referring in practical terms quite simply to the confrontation of an architectural concept with the control of the implementation.[19]

---

15 Alexander Schwarz in conversation with the author on May 12, 2014; see p. 194.
16 Press release on *Mies 1:1* by Robbrecht en Daem architecten (Tine Cooreman), June 2013.
17 "Not only self revelation, but also service!" Mies van der Rohe, notebook entry, undated, Folder 1, The Museum of Modern Art. The Mies van der Rohe Archive, New York. Quoted from Fritz Neumeyer, *Mies van der Rohe. Das kunstlose Wort. Gedanken zur Baukunst*, Berlin, 1986, p. 88.
18 Alexander Schwarz in conversation with the author on May 12, 2014; see p. 196.

Im Gegensatz zum offenen weitläufigen „Saal" gibt Mies dem nach Norden ausgerichteten „Bridgeraum" einen dem Zweck entsprechenden abgeschiedenen Charakter. Die anschließende „Halle" – architektonischer Mittelpunkt der Anlage – bildet den Kreuzungspunkt aller Wege. Hier liegt die Garderobe, der Zugang zum Wirtschaftsbereich, zu einer kleinen Bar und zum Telefonzimmer.

Paul Robbrecht bezeichnet Mies' Golfclub-Entwurf als „missing masterpiece": Entstanden auf dem Höhepunkt von Mies' europäischer Karriere, zeugt er von seiner gereiften architektonischen Sprache, die er souverän handhabt. Er gehört in die Reihe einiger weniger Entwürfe, die zwischen 1928 und 1931 entstanden und Mies' ikonengleiche Bedeutung begründeten: der Barcelona-Pavillon von 1929, Haus Tugendhat in Brünn 1928–1931, das Musterhaus auf der Bauausstellung Berlin 1931 und der Entwurf für Haus Gericke 1932.

Das 1:1-Modell von Robbrecht en Daem architecten   So wie Mies seine Idee von Raum mit wenigen gezielten Linien deutlich formuliert hat, übersetzen Robbrecht en Daem architecten diese Idee mit einer ebenso präzisen minimalistischen Formen- und Materialsprache in ein ephemeres *objet d'architecture* der Gegenwart. Wie Mies selbst stellen auch sie nicht die äußere Erscheinung seiner geplanten Architektur in den Mittelpunkt ihrer Überlegungen, sondern sein architektonisches Konzept. Sie beschreiben den Prozess der Annäherung und Umsetzung als eine Entwicklung „von der unmöglichen Replik zu einem lebensgroßen Modell von Mies' Entwurf"[16]. Nicht Einfühlung und Mutmaßung kennzeichnet ihren Umgang mit den zur Verfügung stehenden Quellen, sondern konstruktive Distanz. „Dienst" statt „Selbstoffenbarung" hätte Mies diese Haltung vielleicht genannt. Den Architekten ging es nicht darum, Mies' Entwurf zu vervollständigen und die fehlenden Informationen „in seinem Sinne" aus anderen Projekten abzuleiten, um ein detailreiches Bild zu schaffen. Bei ihrer Transponierung des Mies'schen Entwurfs in ein 1:1-Modell wird die architektonische Idee zum Orientierungspunkt der Entscheidung, ob und wie, aus welchen Materialien und in welchem Umfang Mies' Vorgaben formuliert werden – und zwar als Architekturmodell, nicht als funktionierendes Gebäude.

Die Umsetzung des Entwurfs von Mies in ein 1:1-Modell eröffnete einen Raum zwischen architektonischer Idee und gebauter Architektur, in dem sich die Freiheit der Zeichnung mit der Kraft der physischen Präsenz verbinden konnte. Nur in diesem Raum war es möglich, einen Schwebezustand zwischen Abstraktion und körperlicher Erfahrbarkeit zu erreichen. Das 1:1-Modell fixierte einen Moment des Übergangs – auf dem Weg zur Vollendung wie der Rohbau oder zur Auflösung wie die Ruine –, in dem die „architektonische Schönheit blank vor einem"[18] liegt. „Es kommt darauf an, wie lang man in der Luft bleibt", sagte Thomas Schütte über den fragilen Prozess der Überführung einer gedachten Architektur in eine gebaute, und meinte damit auch ganz praktisch die Konfrontation eines architektonischen Konzeptes mit der Bauaufsicht.[19]

Es war nicht nötig „zu landen", um das Bild von Schütte fortzusetzen. Die Form des Modells ermöglichte es, Mies' Architektur wie ein Destillat

16 Pressetext zu *Mies 1:1* von Robbrecht en Daem architecten (Tine Cooreman), Juni 2013.
17 „Nicht nur Selbstoffenbarung sondern auch Dienst!" forderte Mies vom Architekten. Mies van der Rohe, Eintragung im Notizbuch o. D., Folder 1, The Museum of Modern Art. The Mies van der Rohe Archive, New York. Zitiert nach: Fritz Neumeyer, *Mies van der Rohe. Das kunstlose Wort. Gedanken zur Baukunst*, Berlin 1986, S. 88.
18 Alexander Schwarz im Gespräch mit der Autorin am 12.5.2014, siehe in diesem Band, S. 197.
19 Thomas Schütte im Gespräch mit Julian Heynen am 15.9.2013 im 1:1-Modell in Krefeld, siehe L.I.S.A.-Portal der Gerda Henkel Stiftung unter www.lisa.gerda-henkel-stiftung.de.

It was not necessary to "land" in order to elaborate on the image provided by Schütte. The form of the model made it possible to exhibit Mies' architecture in distilled form, rather than to let it perform as a kind of costume. "Only skyscrapers which are still being built reveal the bold, constructive thoughts," said Mies in 1922, referring to the design of his glass skyscraper in Berlin.[20]

For the arriving visitor, the 1:1 model is perceived as a flat building of around four meters in height. The eccentric parts of the building stretch from north to south and from east to west over a length of ninety meters [ill. pp. 84–101].

The load-bearing structure of the model accords with the steel-skeleton structure that Mies hinted at in his sketches. The walls and roof are built as wooden constructions and are paneled with white, scoured maritime pine slabs. Only three freestanding wall elements, in the hall and between the entrance area and the terrace, are treated with a surface of clear varnish to emphasize their grain. The various types of treatment are carried out in reference to Mies' preference for valuable wall materials, such as those used in the Barcelona Pavilion and Haus Tugendhat. The flooring is executed in gray concrete slabs with dimensions of 1 x 1 meter. Thin glassless frames hint at the window and door elements; the freestanding wall elements serve to arrange the space.

Mies often only gave outlines of the ancillary areas of the complex, providing just a few references to the room division. Information on the window openings and sill heights either varied or were not available. The design was still at a stage in which the design of these areas played no role. For this reason, in the 1:1 model, these parts of the building are fragmentary: the changing rooms and the trainer area in the south, as well as the housekeeper's quarters in the northern part of the complex, have been carried out without a roof; the flooring slabs have been implemented as gravel, and the framework stands have been left open in some places. In the context of the model, they develop their own almost sculptural effect; this offers an important counterbalance for the suggestive effect of the space of the lobby and the hall [ill. pp. 142–145, 148–149].

The rich grace of the thirty-two visible steel columns of the supporting construction creates an obvious contrast to this minimalism. Representing "false spolia" the columns break up the reduced material language of the model. Paneled with polished high-grade steel, the surfaces reflect the incoming light in all directions, so that the load-bearing function of the supports is dissolved in reflections and light.[21] It is these that allow the final completion of the atmosphere of lightness hinted at in Mies' drawings; they act as a signet, referring to their originator. So it can be said that the general impression of the construction, despite the simplicity of the materials, is one of elegance, radiating a compelling air of tranquility.

It was noticeable that many visitors could not escape the spatial effect of the 1:1 model, regardless of the degree of their previous knowledge. The rhythm of the columns, the wide-framed views, the hall reminiscent of a prostyle: all this radiated an atmosphere that was transferred to the visitors. They described their experience of visiting

19 Thomas Schütte in conversation with Julian Heynen on October 15, 2013, in the 1:1 Model in Krefeld. Online in the L.I.S.A. portal of the Gerda-Henkel-Stiftung under www.lisa.gerda-henkel-stiftung.de.
20 Ludwig Mies van der Rohe, "Hochhäuser", in: *Frühlicht*, Volume 1, Magazine 4, 1922, p. 122.
21 The only element of the model that is made of textile is a white curtain at the west side of the building. This was a technically necessary addition, in order to provide protection to some areas from wind and sunlight during events.

zu zeigen anstatt es als Kostümstück zu inszenieren. „Nur im Bau befindliche Wolkenkratzer zeigen die kühnen konstruktiven Gedanken", so erläuterte Mies 1922 den Entwurf seines Glashochhauses in Berlin.[20]

Dem ankommenden Besucher präsentierte sich das 1:1-Modell als flacher Bau von knapp 4 Metern Höhe. Seine exzentrischen Gebäudeteile erstrecken sich von Norden nach Süden sowie auch von Osten nach Westen über eine Länge von 90 Metern [Abb. S. 84–101].

Das Tragwerk des Modells entspricht der von Mies in seinen Skizzen angedeuteten Stahlskelettstruktur. Wände und Dach sind als Holzständerwerk gebaut und mit weiß geschlämmten Seekieferplatten beplankt. Nur drei frei stehende Wandelemente im „Saal" und zwischen Eingangsbereich und Terrasse erhalten eine Oberfläche aus klarem Lack, wodurch ihre Maserung stärker zutage tritt. Die unterschiedliche Behandlung verweist auf Mies' Vorliebe für kostbare Materialwände, wie er sie auch beim Barcelona-Pavillon und beim Haus Tugendhat eingesetzt hat. Die Bodenflächen sind mit 1 x 1 Meter großen grauen Betonplatten belegt. Schmale Rahmen ohne Glas deuten die Fenster- und Türelemente an, die frei stehenden Wandelemente gliedern den Raum.

Die Nebenbereiche der Anlage hatte Mies in seinen Plänen häufig nur als Volumen umrissen mit wenigen Hinweisen zur Raumaufteilung. Angaben zu Fensteröffnungen und der Höhe der Brüstungen variieren oder lagen nicht vor. Der Entwurf befand sich an einem Punkt, an dem die Gestaltung dieser Bereiche noch keine Rolle spielte. Im 1:1-Modell sind diese Gebäudeteile deshalb fragmentarisch wiedergegeben: Umkleide und Trainerbereich im Süden sowie der Wirtschaftstrakt im nördlichen Teil der Anlage bleiben ohne Dach, Kies ersetzt die Bodenplatten, das Ständerwerk ist in einigen Teilen offen gelassen. Im Kontext des Modells entwickelten sie eine eigene, beinahe skulpturale Wirkung, die ein wichtiges Gegengewicht zur suggestiven Raumwirkung von Halle und Saal darstellt [Abb. S. 142–145, 148–149].

In auffälligem Kontrast zu diesem Minimalismus steht die kostbare Anmutung der 32 sichtbaren Stahlstützen der Tragkonstruktion. Als „falsche Spolien" durchbrechen sie die reduzierte Materialsprache des Modells. Verkleidet mit poliertem Edelstahlblech reflektieren die Oberflächen das einfallende Licht in alle Richtungen, sodass sich die tragende Funktion der Stützen in Spiegelungen und Licht auflöst.[21] Erst durch sie wird die Atmosphäre von Leichtigkeit, die Mies in seinen Zeichnungen andeutete, vollendet, wie ein Signet verweisen sie auf ihren Urheber. So war der Gesamteindruck des Baus trotz der Schlichtheit der Materialien elegant und strahlte eine eindringliche Ruhe aus.

Es ist auffällig, dass sich viele Besucher der Raumwirkung des 1:1-Modells nicht entziehen konnten, unabhängig von ihren Vorkenntnissen. Der Rhythmus der Stützen, die weiten gerahmten Ausblicke, der an ein Prostylos erinnernde Saal verbreiteten eine Atmosphäre, die sich auf die Besucher übertrug. Sie beschreiben ihre Erfahrung beim Besuch des 1:1-Modells als „überwältigend", „ergreifend" und sogar als „magisch". Ist es die „Stimmigkeit", von der Alexander Schwarz mit Verweis auf Heidegger spricht, eine Erfahrung von „Wahrheit", die diese Wahrnehmungen auslöst?[22] Und: Löste der Entwurf Mies van der Rohes diese

20 Ludwig Mies van der Rohe, „Hochhäuser", in: *Frühlicht*, Bd. 1, Heft 4, 1922, S. 122.
21 Das einzige textile Element des Modells, ein weißer Vorhang an der Westseite des Gebäudes, war eine technisch notwendige Ergänzung, um bestimmte Bereiche bei Veranstaltungen gegen Wind und Sonnenlicht schützen zu können.

the 1:1 model as "breathtaking," "moving," and even "magical." Is it the "consistency," which Alexander Schwarz uses to refer to Heidegger— an experience of "truth"—that arouses these observations?[22] Another question was whether it was Mies van der Rohe's design, the 1:1 model, or Mies as modeled by Robbrecht en Daem that caused these experiences.

During the exhibition, three symposia took place within the 1:1 model: art historians, historians, architects, philosophers and artists approached the phenomenon of *Mies 1:1* from various perspectives. Some of these contributions have been reworked and have found their way into this publication; they throw light on the role of architecture as a place in which memories are stored and on the function of the 1:1 model as a precisely directed suggestion of this, and they reflect the "model" as a figure of thinking, an artistic strategy, and a "Möglichkeitsraum" or "space of possibility."

Mies has a great attraction for those studying architecture when it comes to putting the skills involved in classical or digital modeling to the test. Students who visited the 1:1 model asked again and again whether Mies' constructions and designs were particularly suited for implementation as models.

The apparent simplicity of his architecture is particularly visible in the countless post hoc miniatures of the Barcelona Pavilion. The digital reproductions are even more manifold. The more playful versions often offer the most insight: computer-generated images of the pavilion covered with icicles and surrounded by snow drifts, or placed in a sand-dune landscape with deckchairs, or adorned with furniture and wallpaper, show at the very least that the building is tolerant of a great deal of improvisation.[23] However, to make the "Wesen" (essence) of this architecture visible, as Mies might perhaps have expressed it, is beyond the scope of these miniature reproductions, images, and animations. The scope for misunderstanding, with regard to the "tempting simplicity of the Mies structure which does not allow for any presumption of the difficult path of distillation," leads to "simplification and thus exhaustion, which is also the case here."[24]

And yet it is still possible to give an affirmative answer to the question: is Mies' architecture suitable for models? Yes. Not because of its supposed simplicity and clarity, but due to its apodictic character which is also expressed in Mies' commentary on the Golf Club design. Peter Blake already attested that Mies' architecture has the ability "to produce architectural statements of such overwhelming precision, simplicity, and single-mindedness that their impact is that of a major relevation."[25] Fritz Neumeyer added that the written, the drawn, and the built can each be understood as a kind of manifesto, as a demonstration of an idea.[26] His description is particularly applicable to the European work of the architect: that Mies' buildings "as platonic objects seem to announce the essential, timelessly valid principles of architecture."[27] It is probably not so much the apparently simple form of the architecture of Mies van der Rohe that attracts students. Could it be its tranquil finality?

Translated from the German by Joseph Given

22 Alexander Schwarz, see p. 194.
23 Examples can found under Barcelona-Pavillon in the Internet (images and films): e.g. (with snow) www.vi-3d.de/sites/default/files/imagecache/maxgross/pimage/p5_winter.jpg; (with palm trees): www.youtube.com/watch?v=g3Aippf4SQA
24 Fritz Neumeyer, *Mies van der Rohe. Das kunstlose Wort. Gedanken zur Baukunst*, Berlin 1986, p. 14.
25 Peter Blake, *Masterbuilders: Le Corbusier, Mies van der Rohe, Frank Lloyd Wright*, New York 1996 (1960), p. 183.
26 Neumeyer, 1986, p. 11.
27 Ibid., p. 12.

Erfahrungen aus, das 1:1-Modell oder aber der von Robbrecht en Daem modellierte Mies?

Während der Dauer der Ausstellung fanden drei Symposien im 1:1-Modell statt, bei denen sich Kunsthistoriker, Historiker, Architekten, Philosophen und Künstler dem Phänomen *Mies 1:1* aus verschiedenen Richtungen annäherten. Einige Beiträge haben in überarbeiteter Form Eingang in diese Publikation gefunden; sie beleuchten die Rolle von Architektur als Erinnerungsspeicher und die Funktion des Modells als gezielte Inszenierung eines solchen (Winfried Speitkamp) und sie reflektieren das „Modell" als Denkfigur, als künstlerische Strategie und als „Möglichkeitsraum" (Julian Heynen, Alexander Schwarz, Reinhard Wendler).

Auf Studierende der Architektur übt Mies eine große Anziehungskraft aus, wenn es darum geht, die Fertigkeiten im klassischen oder digitalen Modellbau unter Beweis zu stellen. Studenten, die das 1:1-Modell besuchten, fragten wiederholt, ob sich die Bauten und Entwürfe von Mies besonders gut eignen würden, um sie als Modelle umzusetzen.

Die scheinbare Einfachheit seiner Architektur beschert vor allem dem Barcelona-Pavillon zahllose verkleinerte Nachbauten. Noch mannigfaltiger sind die digitalen Reproduktionen, von denen die verspielten noch am erhellendsten sind: Computergenerierte Bilder des Pavillons mit Eiszapfen und Schneeverwehungen oder in einer Dünenlandschaft mit Deckchairs, mit Wohnmöblierung und Tapete zeugen zumindest davon, dass dieser Bau wirklich viel aushält.[23] Das „Wesen" dieser Architektur sichtbar zu machen, wie Mies es vielleicht ausgedrückt hätte, gelingt diesen Miniaturnachbauten, Bildern und Animationen jedoch nicht. Das Missverständnis um die „verführerische Einfachheit der Mies'schen Struktur, die den mühseligen Weg der Destillation nicht ahnen lässt", führt auch hier dazu, dass sie „simplifiziert und damit schließlich verbraucht" wird.[24]

Und trotzdem kann man die Frage nach der Modelltauglichkeit der Mies'schen Architektur bejahen. Nicht wegen ihrer vermeintlichen Einfachheit und Klarheit, sondern aufgrund ihres apodiktischen Charakters, der auch in Mies' Kommentar zum Golfclub-Entwurf zum Ausdruck kommt. Schon Peter Blake attestierte Mies' Architektur die Fähigkeit „zu architektonischen Aussagen von solch überwältigender Genauigkeit, Einfachheit und Zielstrebigkeit zu gelangen, dass ihre Wirkung der einer bedeutenden Offenbarung gleichkommt"[25]. Fritz Neumeyer ergänzte, dass das „Geschriebene wie das Gezeichnete und Gebaute […] sich jeweils auf seine Art als eine Grundsatzerklärung, als Demonstration einer Idee verstehen"[26] lässt. Besonders auf das europäische Werk des Architekten trifft seine Beschreibung von Mies' Bauten als „platonische Objekte, die von essenziellen, zeitlos gültigen Prinzipien des Architektonischen zu künden scheinen"[27] zu.

Wahrscheinlich ist es gar nicht so sehr die vermeintlich einfache Form der Architektur Mies van der Rohes, die die Studenten anzieht. Ist es vielmehr ihre beruhigende Endgültigkeit?

22 Alexander Schwarz im Gespräch mit der Autorin am 12.5.2014, siehe in diesem Band, S. 193.
23 Beispiele finden sich unter dem Stichwort „Barcelona-Pavillon" im Internet (Bilder oder Film).
24 Fritz Neumeyer, *Mies van der Rohe. Das kunstlose Wort. Gedanken zur Baukunst*, Berlin 1986, S. 14.
25 Peter Blake, *Drei Meisterarchitekten: Le Corbusier, Mies van der Rohe, Frank Lloyd Wright*, München 1962, S. 166.
26 Neumeyer 1986, S. 11.
27 Neumeyer 1986, S. 12.

**Michael Dannenmann
Mies 1:1 2013**

Michael Dannenmann
Mies 1:1 2013

Full view from south-west

Gesamtansicht aus Südwesten

Above: bridge room   Below: hall, view to the south

Oben: Bridgeraum   Unten: Saal, Blick nach Süden

Above: terrace, view to south-east towards the changing rooms Below: hall, view to the north

Oben: Terrasse, Blick nach Südosten auf die Umkleide   Unten: Saal, Blick nach Norden

Hall, view to the north

Saal, Ausblick nach Norden

Hall, view to the west

Saal, Ausblick nach Westen

Above: hall, view to the north-west   Below: hall, view to south-west

Oben: Saal, Ausblick nach Nordwesten   Unten: Saal, Ausblick nach Südwesten

Above: lobby, view to the west   Below: hall, view to the north

Oben: Halle, Blick nach Westen   Unten: Saal, Blick nach Norden

Terrace, view to the north

Terrasse, Blick nach Norden

Above: terrace, view to the east   Below: terrace, view to the west

Oben: Terrasse, Blick nach Osten   Unten: Terrasse, Blick nach Westen

Terrace, view to south-east

Terrasse, Blick nach Südosten

Driveway, view to north-west towards the "housekeepers' area"

Zufahrt, Blick nach Nordwesten auf den „Wirtschaftsbereich"

Above: driveway, view to the west   Below: driveway, view to south-east towards the changing rooms

Oben: Zufahrt, Blick nach Westen   Unten: Zufahrt, Blick nach Südosten auf die Umkleide

Terrace, view to the north-west

Terrasse, Blick nach Nordwesten

Figures in a Landscape

Paul Robbrecht   Johannes Robbrecht

<u>Momentum (1)</u>   Le Corbusier completed "his" Villa Savoye in 1927; Konstantin Melnikov built the Rusakov Workers' Club in Moscow in 1927–28; and Giuseppe Terragni designed the Casa del Fascio in Como in 1932. Ludwig Mies van der Rohe himself built the Barcelona Pavilion for the 1929 International Exhibition, and designed Haus Tugendhat in Brno in 1930. It is arguable that Mies conceived the clubhouse for the Krefeld Golf Club during what might be construed as both the "wonder years" of modernist architecture and the high-water mark of his own authentic architectural idiom: during his American period, he hardly applied this fairly fluent approach at all, and symmetry became the basis of his architecture.

<u>Idea</u>   The Krefeld Golf Club never got the clubhouse; it was never realized; it never existed; it was never "experienced."

<u>Partitur</u>   The unique source material for the clubhouse is preserved in The Mies van de Rohe Archives in The Museum of Modern Art in New York. It offers a fascinating insight into both Mies' ambitions and the development of his own architectural language. Yet the drawings and the design intentions they embody are not only clearly intelligible, but also highly

Figuren in einer Landschaft

Paul Robbrecht   Johannes Robbrecht

<u>Momentum (1)</u>   Le Corbusier baut „seine" Villa Savoye 1929–1931, Konstantin Melnikow 1927–1929 in Moskau den Rusakow-Arbeiterclub. Giuseppe Terragni wird im Jahr 1932 die Casa del Fascio in Como entwerfen. Mies van der Rohe selbst führt 1929 für die Weltausstellung den Barcelona-Pavillon aus und baut 1928–1931 Haus Tugendhat in Brno (Brünn). Das von Mies van der Rohe entworfene Golfclubhaus in Krefeld wurde in einer Zeit konzipiert, die man als die Wunderjahre der modernen Architektur bezeichnen kann. Mies van der Rohe befindet sich auf dem Höhepunkt der Entwicklung und endgültigen Ausarbeitung seiner eigenen Architektursprache. Er wird in seiner amerikanischen Zeit sein Konzept des fließenden Raumgefüges kaum noch anwenden; die Symmetrie wird zur Basis seiner Planführung werden.

<u>Idee</u>   Das Golfclubhaus-Projekt in Krefeld wurde niemals ausgeführt. Es hat niemals existiert, es wurde niemals „erfahren".

<u>Partitur</u>   Das einzigartige Material für das Clubhaus wird im Mies van der Rohe Archive des Museum of Modern Art in New York aufbewahrt. Diese Dokumente vermitteln ein aufschlussreiches Bild der Entwicklung der Mies'schen Architektursprache und seiner Absichten.

suggestive. What he wanted to achieve with the clubhouse in Krefeld was not clearly defined; nor were the drawings at a stage in which the complete architectural project had been precisely defined.

The project was unfinished; it was a work in progress.

There are several ground plans, for instance, each of which sets out the same architectural configuration, but contains minor (and some less minor) differences in each case. Just one cross-section was produced and there are no elevations. Very few measurements are given in the plans but—taking into account the extremely pure perspective views, which provide an absolutely clear picture—we can form an idea of the spatiality, proportionality, and underlying relationships Mies van der Rohe had in mind.

The perspective views show spaces that are entirely empty, apart from the picture of a car near the entrance canopy in one drawing, and a reclining sculpture on a plinth on the terrace side in another. The sculpture vaguely recalls a figure from the pediments of the Parthenon, juxtaposing the mechanistic New Era with the Timeless Classical in a few sketched lines.

Together, this body of drawings of the Krefeld Golf Clubhouse formed the basis for a series of ideas and final choices of how the scale model could be built. It is extremely satisfying to read the plans in the manner of a conductor working through a musical score, setting out emphases, rhythm, and flow. As you read, a musical architecture takes shape in your mind.

<u>Open questions</u> None of the documents makes any reference to use of materials. At this point the project existed in a world of total abstraction.

The "architectonic essay" proved exceptionally successful in focusing and combining three components: the landscape, the constructed space, and the human element. The presence of the latter turned out to be undeniably crucial when the model was finally built.

Does the 1:1 model of the Golf Clubhouse deserve a place in Mies van der Rohe's "official" oeuvre? Is it an addition to the highly limited catalogue of pre-war Mies projects? Or is it rather a manifestation of our interpretations, conjecture and modus operandi in seeking to study Mies van der Rohe's architectural oeuvre?

Our aim was to make it possible to experience the essence of Mies van der Rohe's clubhouse project. "The Reconstruction of an Architectural Idea." We were convinced that building this 1:1 scale model would reveal the "Miesian" space. We wanted to concentrate purely on the essence.

Die Zeichnungen und die darin vermittelten Entwurfsideen sind nicht immer verständlich, sie deuten vieles nur an. Was Mies van der Rohe mit diesem Golfclubhaus in Krofeld ausführen wollte, ist nicht eindeutig. Die Entwürfe befinden sich noch nicht in einem Zustand, der das vollständige architektonische Projekt präzise umreißen würde.

Der Entwurf war unfertig. Es war ein im Werden begriffenes Projekt.

Es gibt verschiedene Grundrisse, die allesamt die gleiche Architekturkonfiguration beschreiben, sie enthalten jedoch immer auch kleine (und nicht so kleine) Unterschiede. Nur ein einziger Schnitt durch das Gebäude ist erhalten. Aufrisse der Fassaden fehlen. Auf den Plänen gibt es kaum Maßangaben. Trotzdem ermöglichen die äußerst sauberen Perspektivzeichnungen eine klare Vorstellung von Räumlichkeit, Proportionalität und zugrunde liegenden Beziehungen in der Raumentwicklung: so wie sie Ludwig Mies van der Rohe vor Augen hatte.

Wenn man von einem abgebildeten Auto in der Nähe des Eingangsvordachs und einer liegenden Skulptur auf einem Sockel an der Terrassenseite absieht, zeigen die unterschiedlichen Perspektiven absolut leere Räume. Die Skulptur erinnert vage an eine Figur aus dem Ziergiebel des Parthenon; die mechanistische Neuzeit nimmt Bezug auf die zeitlose Klassik, die in ein paar skizzierten Linien enthalten ist.

Insgesamt bildete dieses Bündel an Zeichnungen des Golfclubhauses die Grundlage für eine Reihe von Gedankengängen und endgültigen Entscheidungen darüber, wie ein maßstabsgetreues Modell gebaut werden könnte. Genauso wie ein Dirigent Partituren liest und Akzente setzt, Nuancen, Rhythmus und die fließende Bewegung erkennt, so bewirkt auch die Durchsicht dieses Planmaterials eine große Faszination: Beim Lesen dieser Partitur entwickelt sich im Kopf des Architekten bereits ein musikalisches Raumgefüge.

<u>Offene Fragen</u>   Keines der Dokumente erwähnt Mies van der Rohes Vorstellungen des zu verwendenden Materials. Der Entwurf existierte zu diesem Zeitpunkt einzig in einer Welt der absoluten Abstraktion.

Der „architektonische Essay" musste sich deshalb auf drei Komponenten und deren Verbindung konzentrieren: auf Landschaft, konstruierten Raum und den Menschen. Die Anwesenheit des Menschen würde sich später – im gebauten Zustand – auf überraschende Weise als fundamental erweisen.

Geht das 1:1-Modell des Golfclubhauses in das Œuvre von Mies van der Rohe ein? Bildet es eine Ergänzung zu dem schmalen Katalog seiner Projekte zwischen den Weltkriegen? Oder handelt es sich doch eher um eine Manifestation unserer Interpretationen und Vermutungen sowie unseres Modus Operandi, das architektonische Œuvre von Mies van der Rohe zu deuten?

<u>Residue</u> The construction of the model describes the moment when an idea, previously given shape only in drawings, becomes a space that can be experienced physically. The 1:1 model describes the moment before the final decisions would have to be taken: the instant in a design process when it was still purely about the constructed space.

Anything that was not clear in the plans and drawings, we did not build. A building without facades. We left out certain elements of the construction, either because they would not have contributed significantly to the architectural experience, or for economic reasons. A building without a roof.

The end result would be something like a building in progress, or one in the process of being dismantled: a ruin, a torso. The non-construction of certain elements took on a dynamic of its own in the overall working process.

<u>Momentum (2)</u> The 1:1 model was erected temporarily: the project could only be visited for a few months (from May 29, 2013 to October 27, 2014). This non-permanent character lent the Krefeld project an extraordinary momentum—it was something that existed and then disappeared forever. All that now remains is the memory and the documentation.

In this way, the 1:1 Krefeld model indirectly—yet unavoidably—recalls the Barcelona Pavilion, which was built as a temporary structure for the World Exhibition in 1929 and was duly demolished in 1930 before being reconstructed, this time permanently, fifty years later. Where a (seemingly) precise reconstruction was opted for in Barcelona, abstraction was preferred in Krefeld.

<u>Essay</u> The model did not set out in any way to be an actually constructed clubhouse for a golf course. On the contrary, it was to present itself in every respect as a prototype, a model, an exercise, or a three-dimensional structure, the aim of which was to explore and, if possible, reveal Ludwig Mies van der Rohe's architectural thinking.

There were, after all, two aspects: the approach taken by the curator, architects, engineers, and builders, comprising an in-depth study of how to do justice to this unbuilt Mies van der Rohe masterpiece; and the question of how this architectural experiment could in itself achieve an identity and a degree of autonomy.

If the full-scale model was not a building, it was definitely architecture: an *objet d'architecture*, an architectonic construction with its own *raison d'être*.

<u>Zeit</u> Es war unsere Absicht, den Versuch zu unternehmen, das Wesentliche von Mies van der Rohes Golfclub Projekt erlebbar zu machen. „Die Rekonstruktion eines architektonischen Gedankens". Wir waren davon überzeugt, dass wir durch den Bau dieses Modells im Maßstab 1:1 den „Mies'schen" Raum veranschaulichen könnten. Wir wollten uns ausschließlich auf das Wesentliche konzentrieren.

<u>Überreste</u> Das 1:1-Modell markiert den Zeitpunkt, ab dem eine in einzelnen Zeichnungen formulierte Idee zum erfahrbaren Raum wurde. Es markiert zugleich den Augenblick, ab dem endgültige Entscheidungen getroffen werden mussten. Den Zeitpunkt im Entwurfsprozess, ab dem es nur noch um den konstruierten Raum ging.

Was in den Plänen und Zeichnungen nicht ausformuliert worden ist, das haben wir auch nicht gebaut: Ein Modell ohne Fassaden. Bestimmte konstruktive Teile haben wir weggelassen, weil sie zum architektonischen Erleben nur wenig beigetragen hätten. Auch ökonomische Erwägungen spielten eine Rolle: Ein Modell ohne Dächer.

Das Endergebnis sollte so etwas wie ein sich im Aufbau befindliches Gebäude sein; oder auch im Zustand des Abrisses: eine Ruine, ein Torso. Das Weglassen einzelner Teile – das Skizzenhafte – verlieh dem gesamten Werkprozess seine eigene Dynamik.

<u>Momentum (2)</u> Das 1:1-Modell wurde für einen begrenzten Zeitraum errichtet. Nur wenige Monate (von Mai bis Oktober 2013) war es möglich, das Modell zu besuchen. Diese zeitliche Begrenztheit verlieh dem Projekt ein besonderes Momentum: Etwas, das vorübergehend dagewesen ist und dann für immer verschwunden bleibt. Alles was bleibt sind Erinnerung und die verbliebenen Dokumente.

Indirekt – dies war unvermeidlich – spiegelt sich das 1:1-Modell von Krefeld im Barcelona-Pavillon wider. Dieser wurde 1929 im Rahmen der Weltausstellung in Barcelona als temporärer Pavillon erbaut und anschließend wieder demontiert, um dann, gut 50 Jahre später, erneut – und diesmal auf unbestimmte Zeit – aufgebaut zu werden. Während man in Barcelona eine (anscheinend) exakte Rekonstruktion baute, entschied man sich in Krefeld für die Abstraktion, eine temporäre Vergegenwärtigung.

<u>Essay</u> Das Modell sollte keineswegs ein real gebautes Golfclubhaus sein. Vielmehr ein Werkstück, ein Modell, eine Übung, eine dreidimensionale Konstruktion, die das architektonische Denken Ludwig Mies van der Rohes untersuchen und möglichst auch sichtbar machen sollte.

Tatsächlich stellten sich Kuratorin, Architekten, Ingenieure und Fachleute im Vorfeld die Frage, wie dieses nie gebaute Meisterwerk von Mies van der Rohe korrekt ausgeführt werden könnte. Gleichzeitig wurde darüber nachgedacht, wie dieser architektonische Versuch an sich eine Identität und ein gewisses Maß an Autonomie verkörpern könnte.

<u>Unit of measurement</u> The open floor plan comprised a strict grid of 1 x 1 meter elements, to be implemented with the use of concrete slabs.

<u>Structure</u> Mies' spatial conception is not tectonic: the purpose of his flat ceilings, freestanding walls, and differentiated walls was to achieve a sense of full and immanent spatiality, extending out into the infinite landscape.

Our task was to work out how we could go about erecting this temporary, full-size model, with its 87 x 92 meter footprint.

The perspective views show a flat, continuous ceiling and a grid of tiles for the floor, between which columns are installed, with neither bases nor capitals. It is clear that columns with a cross-shaped section were to be used here, like those seen previously in the Barcelona Pavilion and Haus Tugendhat in Brno.

Several solitary walls were positioned very specifically on the 1 x 1 meter grid, defining a sequence of spaces and landscapes. The walls governed the view. The extensive wall surface was supported by slender columns on a 7 x 7 meter grid, tentacling toward a series of canopies and ample eaves. There is no indication in any of the drawings, however, as to how the columns were to be linked to one another by beams. Notwithstanding the temporary nature of the construction, the magnitude of the project led to the choice of a dense steel structure with foundations.

Anomalies in column sections echoed differences in the structural load and were already indicated in Mies' ground plans. The large entrance canopy with its central row of columns, which also have larger sections, are offset with respect to the 7 x 7 meter grid.

The different rows of columns form a vertical cadence in an emphatically sprawling horizontal building.

<u>Abstraction</u> It was decided to use plywood for the walls and all that was enclosed within them. This material, which doesn't feature anywhere in Mies' vocabulary unless we count the wooden panelling in his American work, was used for the surfaces of both the external and internal walls. It was painted translucent white as part of the overall sense of abstraction.

<u>Model</u> There was also a preliminary model, on a scale of 1:200 rather than full size. It was experimentally exhibited at Haus Lange from July 1–3, 2011. We also viewed the plywood used to construct the 1:1 model as a kind of modelling medium. The material was intended to emphasize the temporary nature of models, while also distancing the project from any possible hypothesis regarding an unknown final result.

War das so realitätsnahe Modell zwar kein Gebäude, so handelte es sich dabei doch durchaus um Architektur: um ein *objet d'architecture*, eine architektonische Konstruktion, die ihre Daseinsberechtigung in sich selbst findet.

 Maßeinheit Der offene Grundriss basiert auf einem starren Raster von 1 x 1 Meter. Sichtbar ist dies auf dem Boden, der mit großen Betonplatten ausgeführt ist.

 Struktur Das Raumbild von Mies ist nicht tektonisch, vielmehr will er mit seinen Flachdächern, den frei stehenden Wandelementen und den Materialwänden eine immanente Räumlichkeit entstehen lassen, die sich in der endlosen Landschaft fortsetzt.

Für uns ging es um die konkrete Frage, wie wir dieses temporäre maßstabsgetreue Modell errichten könnten. Immerhin würde es sich auf einer Fläche von fast 87 x 92 Metern erstrecken.

Die Perspektivzeichnungen zeigen eine flache, durchgehende Decke und einen gerasterten Fußboden. Dazwischen entwickelt sich das Raster des Tragwerks, sichtbar durch die Stützen im Abstand von 7 x 7 Metern. Aus den Zeichnungen lässt sich lesen, dass Mies hier die gleichen Stützen mit kreuzförmigem Querschnitt verwenden wollte wie bereits im Barcelona-Pavillon und Haus Tugendhat in Brno (Brünn).

Auf dem 1 x 1 Meter-Gitter positionierte Mies gezielt eine Reihe von frei stehenden Wänden, sodass eine Sequenz von Räumen und Landschaften entsteht. Die Wände lenken den Blick. Die ausgedehnte Dachfläche wird von schlanken Stützen mit einem Rastermaß von 7 x 7 Metern getragen. Keine der (historischen) Zeichnungen zeigt, wie diese Stützen mittels Träger verbunden sind. Trotz des temporären Charakters der Konstruktion wurde aufgrund der Dimensionen dieses Projektes eine fundamentierte feste Stahlstruktur gewählt.

Abweichungen der Stützenstellungen finden ihre Begründung in Unterschieden der strukturellen Last; sie waren bereits in den Grundrissen von Mies zu erkennen. Das große Empfangsvordach mit der zentralen Reihe von Stützen ist hinsichtlich des 7 x 7-Rasters verschoben platziert.

Die Stützenreihen bilden eine vertikale Kadenz in einem ansonsten weiträumigen horizontalen Gebäude.

 Abstraktion Im Laufe der Planung wurde entschieden, für die Wände Sperrholz einzusetzen – ein Material, das im Vokabular von Mies gar nicht vorkommt (sofern man von hölzernen Täfelungen in seinem amerikanischen Œuvre absieht). Dieses Sperrholz wird sowohl außen als auch innen für die Verkleidungen des Ständerwerks verwendet und wurde weiß geschlämmt, um eine stärkere Abstraktion zu erreichen.

The 1:1 scale model was intended more to capture a moment or an intention at a particular phase of the project. It was a prototype that could only focus on a few aspects. We deliberately departed from the concept of abstraction on two points.

<u>Highlighting (1)</u> The preciousness of the original cross-shaped profile sections—steel, covered with chrome plate—was indicated in the scale model through the use of highly polished stainless steel plate.

<u>Highlighting (2)</u> An exception was made for a few special walls. Mies van der Rohe probably intended to use a high-quality, durable material for the solitary walls, which have a spatially defining function and contribute emphatically to both the revealing and concealing of the landscape: something like the onyx or marble he used in Brno or Barcelona.

The story goes that Mies developed an interest in ethnic African domestic cultures, in which lengths of brightly coloured fabric, decorated with geometric motifs, were hung around a settlement as a token of welcome. The walls, with their sawn stone slabs, contributed to a welcoming environment. In the 1:1 model they were left unpainted and were finished instead with a glossy varnish that sharply accentuated the wood grain.

Loos once said that sawing through stone reveals the material's soul, and something similar happens when wood is cut into thin layers to turn it into "common or garden" plywood.

<u>Mies</u> Mies van der Rohe's architectural works are *Weltbilder*. They distil a view of the world that is full of clarity, and free from any totalitarian utopia or stage-management of human existence. They position the individual in space and give him the confidence and freedom—but also the responsibility—to grasp the complexity and constant changes around him.

They refer to an immense landscape with an astonishing abundance of possibilities and questions.

<u>The wind rose</u> When the 1:1 scale model of Mies van der Rohe's Golf Clubhouse had been built, it revealed a remarkable phenomenon: the surrounding landscape was precisely defined and given an identity. The vagueness of nature—in Krefeld's case the nature reserve "am Engelsberg"—is once again delineated. The orthogonal character of the wind rose plan almost literally marked the spot with a cross.

Two galleries positioned perpendicularly to one another, the entrance canopy and the space in front of the changing rooms, continue into the overall configuration of the linked spaces. It is hard to shed the sense that this geometrical figure extends infinitely into the landscape.

<u>Maquette</u>   Das erste Modell war nicht im Maßstab 1:1, sondern in 1:200. Ein Versuch in Balsaholz, der im Haus Lange vom 1. bis zum 3. Juli 2011 ausgestellt wurde. Auch das Sperrholz, aus dem das endgültige 1:1-Modell gebaut wurde, war für uns ein derartiges Modellmaterial. Das Material sollte die zeitliche Begrenztheit des Modells hervorheben. Mit dem Einsatz von Sperrholz sollte jegliche Hypothese über das mögliche Aussehen des Golfclubhauses vermieden werden.

Das Modell im Maßstab 1:1 wollte eher den Zeitpunkt und die Intention einer bestimmten Planungsphase festhalten. Insofern handelte es sich um einen Prototyp, der sich auf einzelne Aspekte konzentrieren musste. An zwei Stellen wurde der Weg der Abstraktion gezielt verlassen:

<u>Hervorhebung (1)</u>   Die Kostbarkeit der ursprünglich mit Chromblech verkleideten stählernen Kreuzprofile wird im 1:1-Modell durch die Verwendung von hochglanzpoliertem rostfreiem Stahlblech veranschaulicht.

<u>Hervorhebung (2)</u>   Auch bei einigen Wänden wird eine Ausnahme gemacht. Für die frei stehenden Wandelemente mit raumbestimmendem Charakter hätte Mies van der Rohe möglicherweise ein hochwertigeres, dauerhafteres Material einsetzen wollen. Denn sie wirken beim Sichtbarmachen und Verbergen der Landschaft selbstbewusst mit. Mies dachte hier wahrscheinlich beispielsweise an Onyx oder Marmor, wie er es auch in Brno (Brünn) oder Barcelona verwendete.

Man erzählt sich ja, dass Mies van der Rohe Interesse an ethnischen Wohnkulturen Afrikas gefunden hatte, bei denen Tücher mit grell-geometrischen Motiven als Begrüßungszeichen rings um die Siedlungen aufgehängt wurden. Die Mauern mit ihren gesägten Natursteinplatten tragen in sich etwas von einem Ambiente, in dem man freundliche Aufnahme findet. Im 1:1-Modell bleiben diese Mauern unbemalt und werden mit Hochglanz-Firnis versehen, sodass die Zeichnung des Holzes sehr stark akzentuiert wird.

Adolf Loos zufolge macht das Durchsägen von Naturstein die Seele des Materials sichtbar. Etwas Ähnliches geschieht auch, wenn man Holz in dünne Schichten schneidet, um daraus das „ganz gewöhnliche" Sperrholz zu machen.

<u>Mies</u>   Mies van der Rohes Architekturen sind „Weltbilder", sie verdichten die Einsicht in die Welt mit einer Klarheit, die jeglicher totalitären Utopie und der Lenkung des menschlichen Daseins abgeneigt ist. Sie positionieren das Individuum innerhalb eines Raumes und geben ihm sowohl Selbstbewusstsein und Freiheit als auch Verantwortlichkeit, um einen Einblick in die Komplexität und die sich fortwährend vollziehenden Veränderungen zu erhalten.

The underlying cross figure never becomes overbearing, and the plan opens up freely into the context of the natural surroundings.

An unexpected complexity and experience develops, however, when one walks toward the building below the canopy. The deeper view is concealed by a diagonal, confronting wall that was present from Mies' first sketches—a theatrical gesture that makes the revelation of the landscape beyond all the more intense. A three-dimensional configuration of freestanding walls orients the gaze and establishes the spatial continuum of the main hall, the conference room, and the terrace.

The field of vision now follows two directions. The first indicates a possible route for golfers to follow, while the other fixes on the landscape scene. A golf clubhouse is, after all, an observation post: a pavilion offering a panoramic view, an opportunity to observe and study the play. The game unfolds in the landscape, marking out and exploring its boundaries. The sport of golf unites precise measuring and force.

Golfers in a landscape.

<u>Figures in a landscape</u> The visitors to the 1:1 scale model were not, however, golfers, but people interested in Mies van der Rohe and in a spatial, architectural essay. Spectators. Yet there were also chance passers-by: people walking their dogs, joggers, cyclists, and horse riders. Actors. Little scenes arose, developed, or repeated themselves.

The degree to which the second group became the first, or vice versa, was not always clear.

<u>Epilogue</u>   Everything changes at the moment of actual experience. The necessity of the spatial essay, the model, was further intensified by its temporary character. This was the moment of a project that hitherto only existed in the archives.

The knowledge obtained by constructing the 1:1 model was incisive: through the research, the construction, and ultimately the physical experience of this "walkable" architectural object. Yet it also left all sorts of uncertainties behind. Visible ones. Nothing was brought to a conclusion.

May 2014

Translated from the Dutch by Ted Alkins

Sie beziehen sich auf eine unermessliche Landschaft mit erschreckend vielen Möglichkeiten und Fragestellungen.

<u>Windrose</u>   Als das Modell von Mies van der Rohes Golfclubhaus im Maßstab 1:1 gebaut ist, zeigt sich ein merkwürdiges Phänomen: Die Landschaft ringsum wird präzisiert und erhält eine Identität. Die Unbestimmtheit der Natur – in diesem Fall das Landschaftsschutzgebiet am Engelsberg bei Krefeld – wird auf einmal gegliedert. Durch die Orthogonalität des Gebäudes wird der Ort buchstäblich mit einem Kreuz markiert.

Zwei im rechten Winkel zueinander stehende Galerien, das Eingangsvordach und das Vordeck der Umkleideräume, setzen sich in der Gesamtkonfiguration der miteinander verbundenen Räume fort. Man wird das Gefühl nicht los, dass sich diese geometrische Figur in der Landschaft endlos fortsetzt. Die zugrunde liegende Kreuzfigur ist nirgendwo zwingend, und der Plan öffnet sich frei hin zum umgebenden Landschaftskontext.

Jedoch entfaltete sich eine unerwartete Komplexität und ein unerwartetes Erleben, wenn man unter dem Vordach zum Gebäude hin spazierte. Die Sicht auf die Landschaft wird durch eine quer verlaufende, frei stehende Wand versperrt, die bereits in den ersten Skizzen von Mies zu finden ist. Diese theatralische Geste macht die dahinter liegende Offenbarung der Landschaft nur noch intensiver. Durch die räumliche Konfiguration der frei stehenden Wände erhält der Blick Orientierung; auf diese Weise entsteht das Raumkontinuum der Halle, des großen Saales und der Terrasse.

Das Blickfeld dehnt sich in zwei Richtungen aus. Während die eine Blickrichtung sich auf den Weg bezieht, dem die Golfspieler möglicherweise folgen, beruht die andere auf der landschaftlichen Szenerie. Ein Golfclubhaus ist schließlich ein Beobachtungsposten. Ein Panoramapavillon. Von hier aus will man das Spiel beobachten und studieren. Dieses Spiel entwickelt sich innerhalb der Landschaft. Es misst sie ab und untersucht ihre Grenzen. Das Golfspiel vereint in seiner Spielweise Vermessen und Kräfte.

Golfspieler in einer Landschaft.

<u>Figuren in einer Landschaft</u>   Die Besucher des 1:1-Modells waren jedoch keine Golfspieler. Es handelte sich in erster Linie um Menschen, die sich für Mies van der Rohe und den räumlichen architektonischen Essay interessierten: Zuschauer. Es gab auch zufällige Passanten, Spaziergänger mit Hunden, Jogger, Radfahrer und Reiter: Darsteller. Kleine Szenen entwickelten sich, wurden weitergesponnen oder wiederholten sich.

Das Ausmaß, in dem sich diese zweite Gruppe in die erste verwandelte (oder auch umgekehrt), war nicht immer ganz deutlich zu erkennen.

<u>Epilog</u> Alles verändert sich im Augenblick des tatsächlichen Erlebens. Die Notwendigkeit des räumlichen Essays – des 1:1-Modells – wurde durch die zeitliche Begrenztheit noch verstärkt. Es war der Moment eines Projektes, das bisher lediglich in den Archiven existiert hatte.
Die Erfahrungen, die die Konstruktion des 1:1-Modells mit sich brachte, waren tiefgreifend – sowohl in der Untersuchung als auch beim Aufbau und letztendlichen Erleben dieses begehbaren Architekturobjektes. Sie hinterließen jedoch auch viele Unsicherheiten. Und diese waren sichtbar. Nichts wurde zu Ende geführt.

Mai 2014

Aus dem Niederländischen übersetzt von Klaus Roth

**Robbrecht en
Daem architecten
Mies 1:1**

Robbrecht en
Daem architecten
Mies 1:1

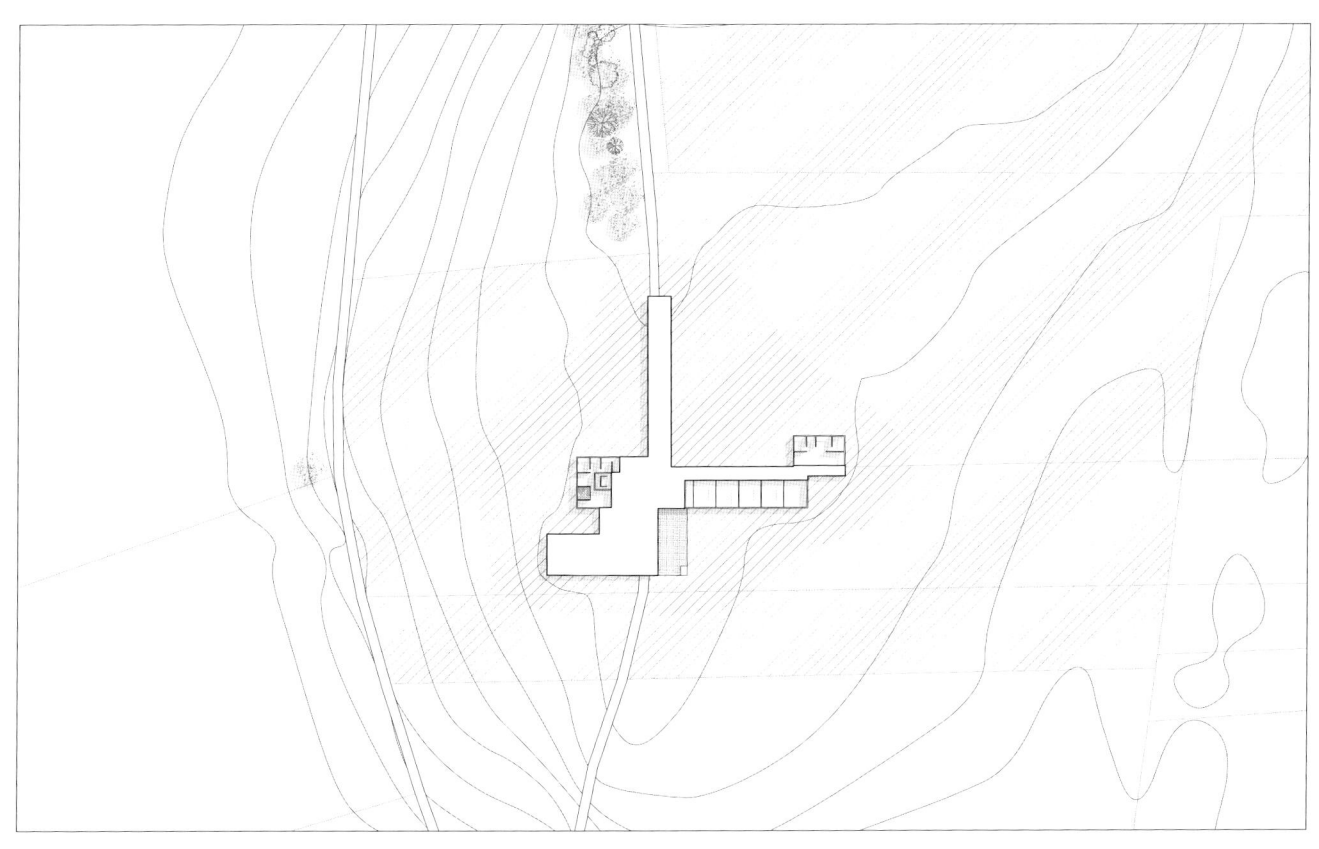

Site plan

Lageplan

1 **Housekeeping area** Eingang
2 **Trainer area** Wirtschaftsbereich
3 **Hall** Saal
4 **Terrace** Terrasse
5 **Changing rooms** Umkleide

a. **Entrance** Eingang
b. **Lobby** Halle
c. **Telephone** Telefonzimmer
d. **Bar** Bar
e. **Housekeepers' dwelling** Wirtschafterwohnung
f. **Wardrobe** Garderobe
g. **Kitchen** Küche
h. **Patio** Wirtschaftshof
i. **Bridge room** Bridgeraum
j. **Sculpture** Skulptur
k. **Caddies** Caddy
l. **Shop and workshop** Verkaufsraum
m. **Trainer's unit** Trainerwohnung

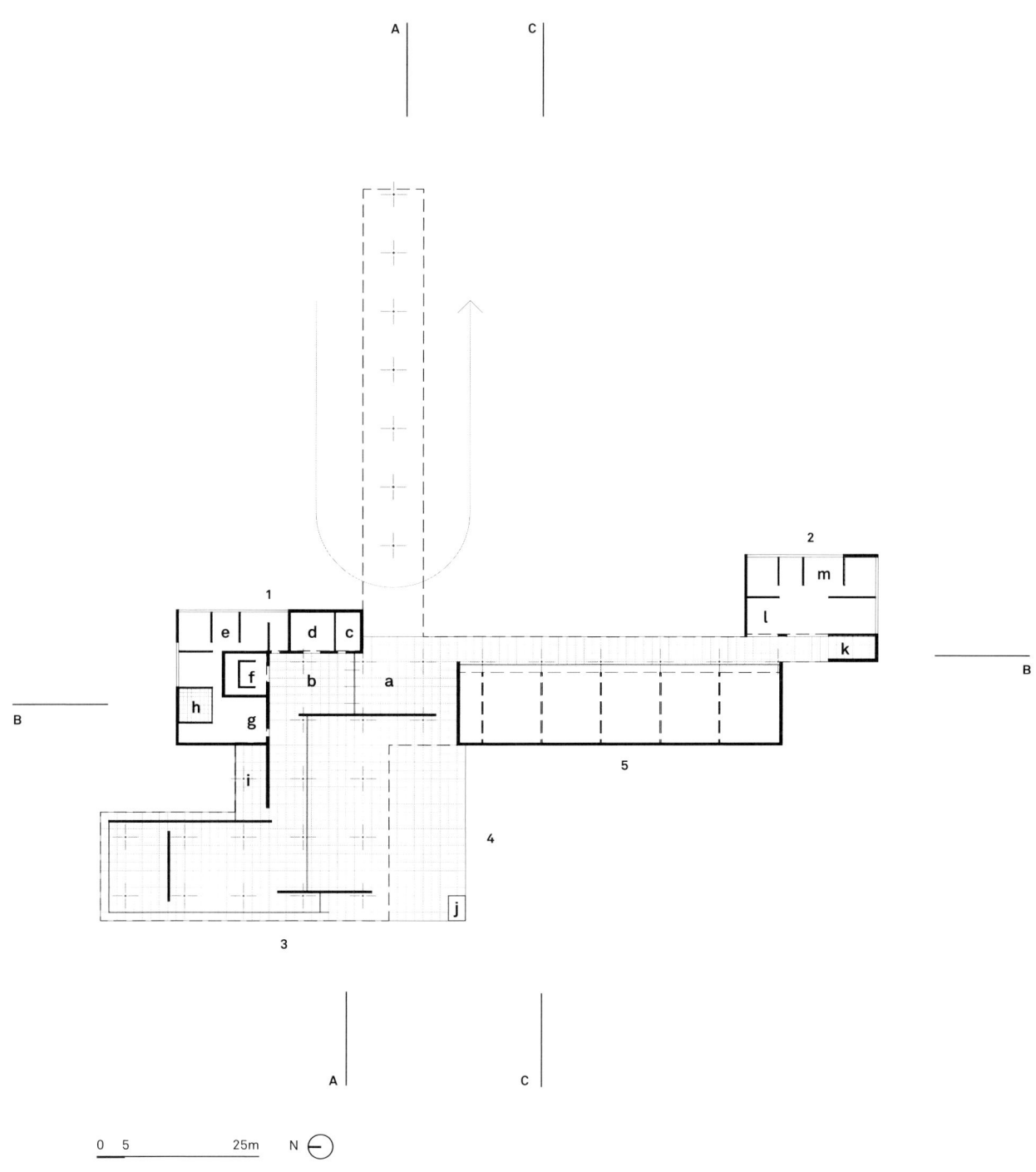

Ground floor plan

Grundriss Erdgeschoss

West elevation Westansicht

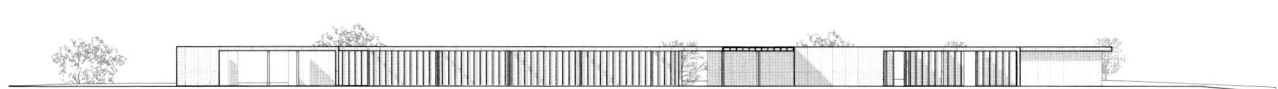

East elevation Ostansicht

South elevation Südansicht

North elevation Nordansicht

0　10　　25 m

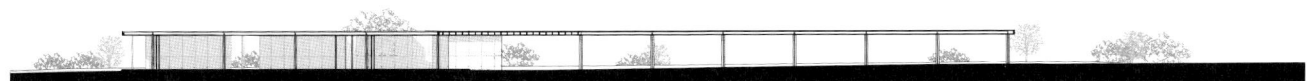

Section AA Schnitt AA

Section BB Schnitt BB

Section CC Schnitt CC

0 10 25 m

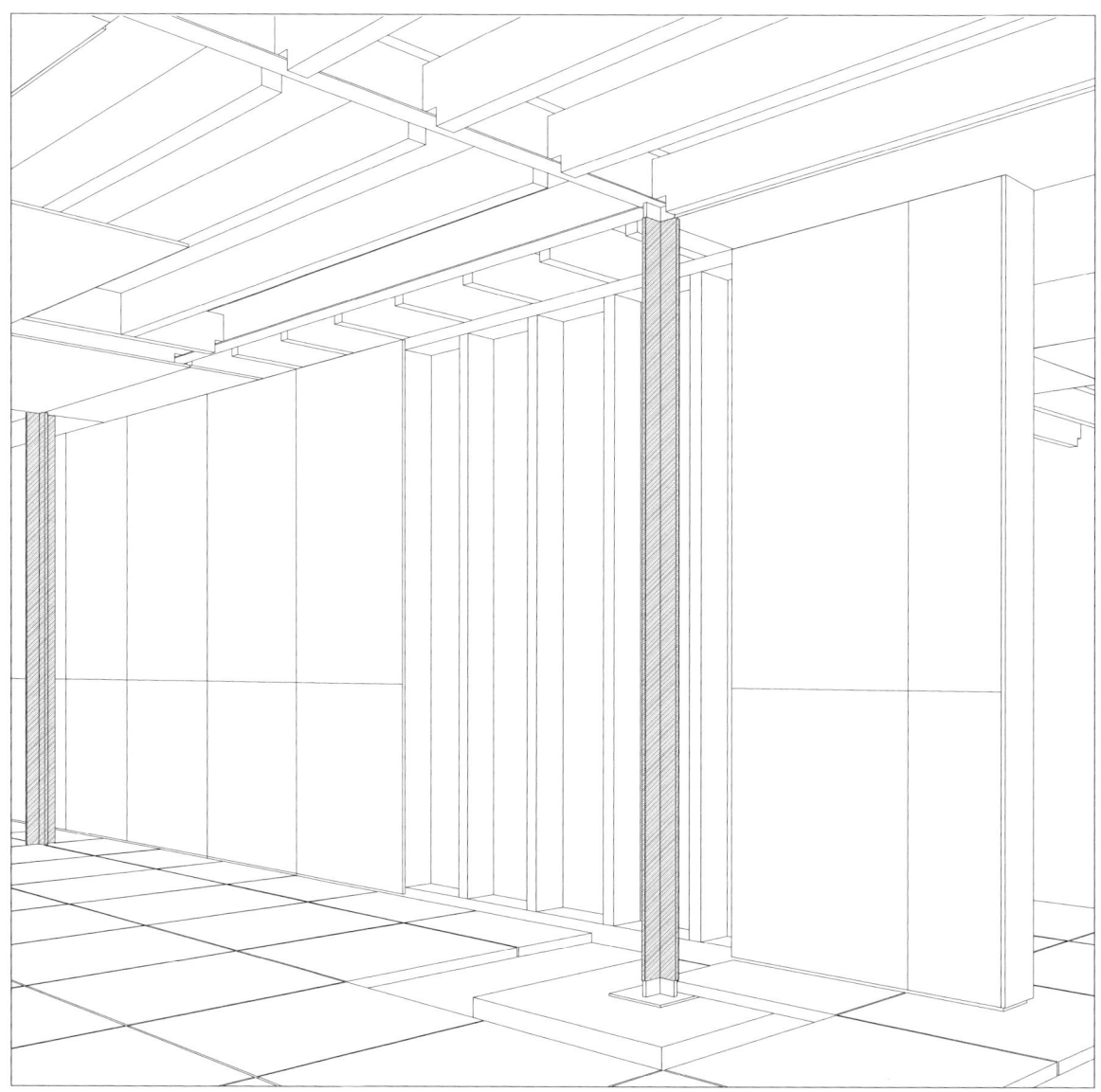

Construction detail

Konstruktionsdetail

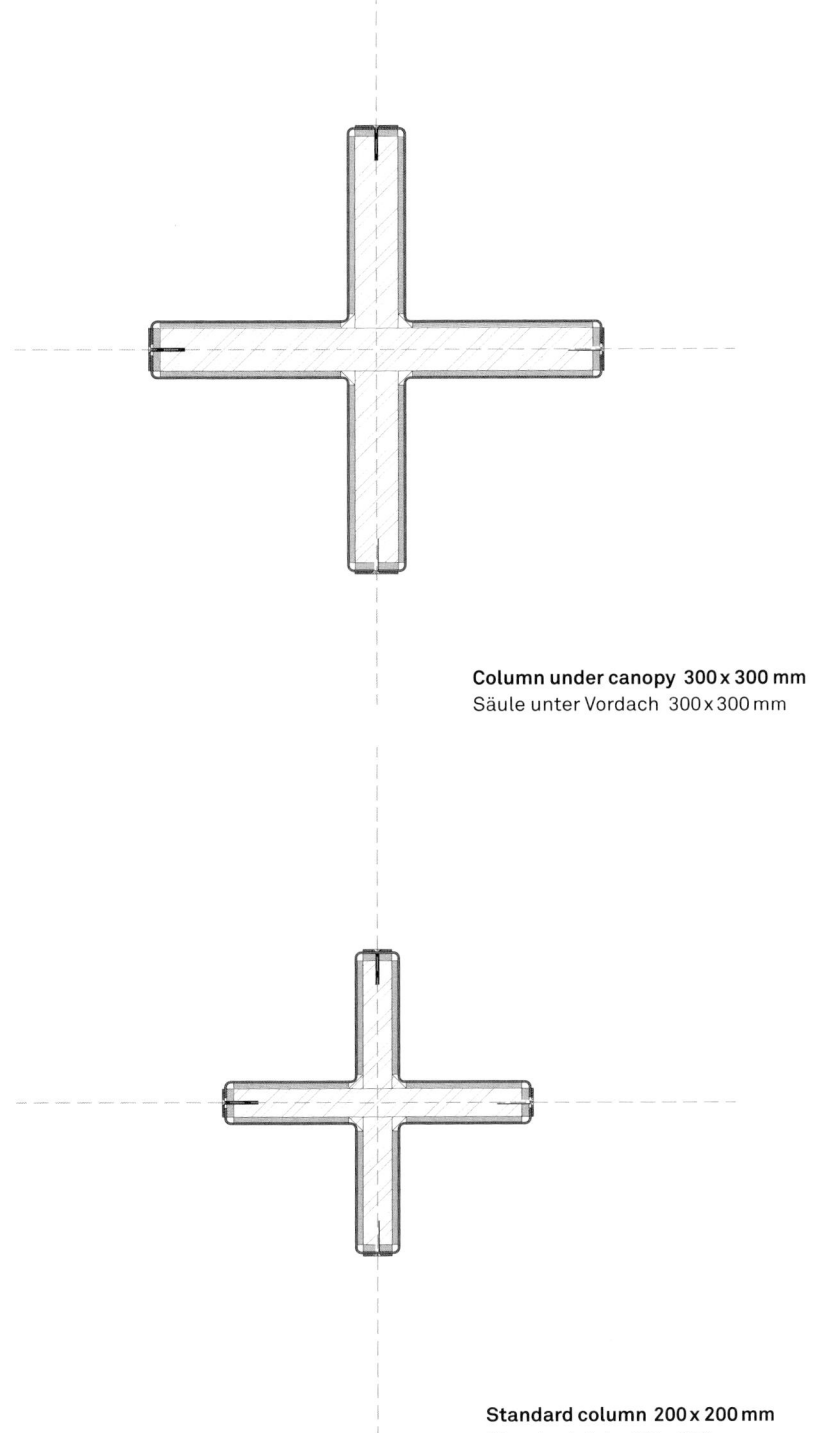

Column under canopy 300 x 300 mm
Säule unter Vordach 300 x 300 mm

Standard column 200 x 200 mm
Standardsäule 300 x 300 mm

Column details

Säulendetails

South-east Süd-Ost

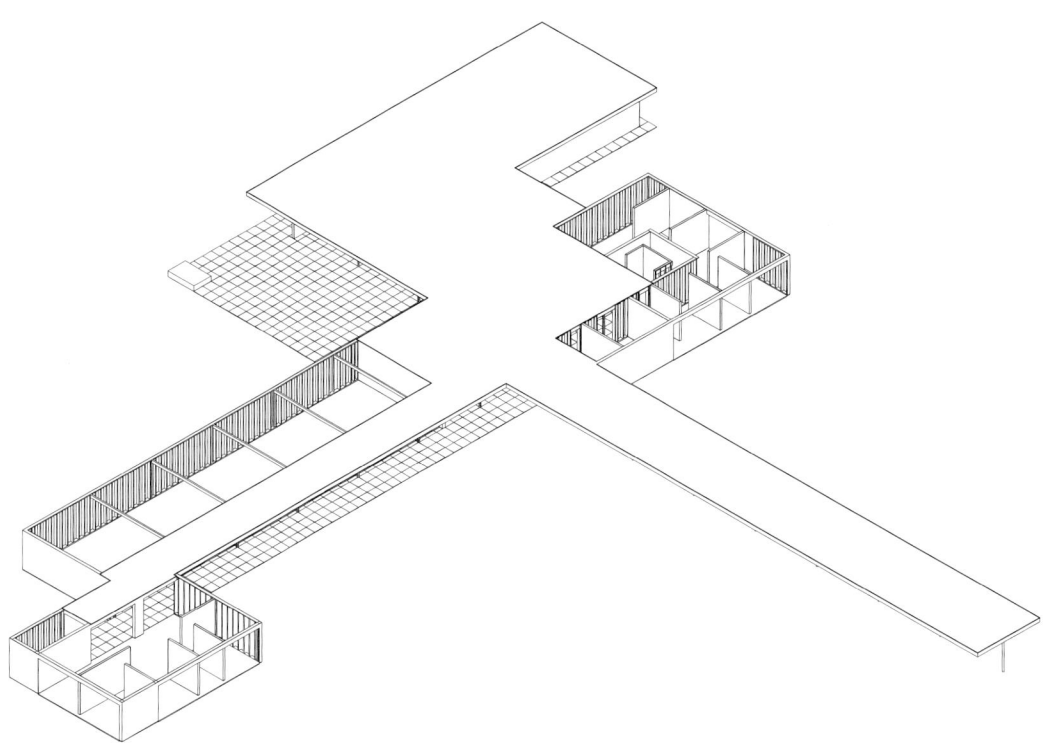

North-west Nord-West

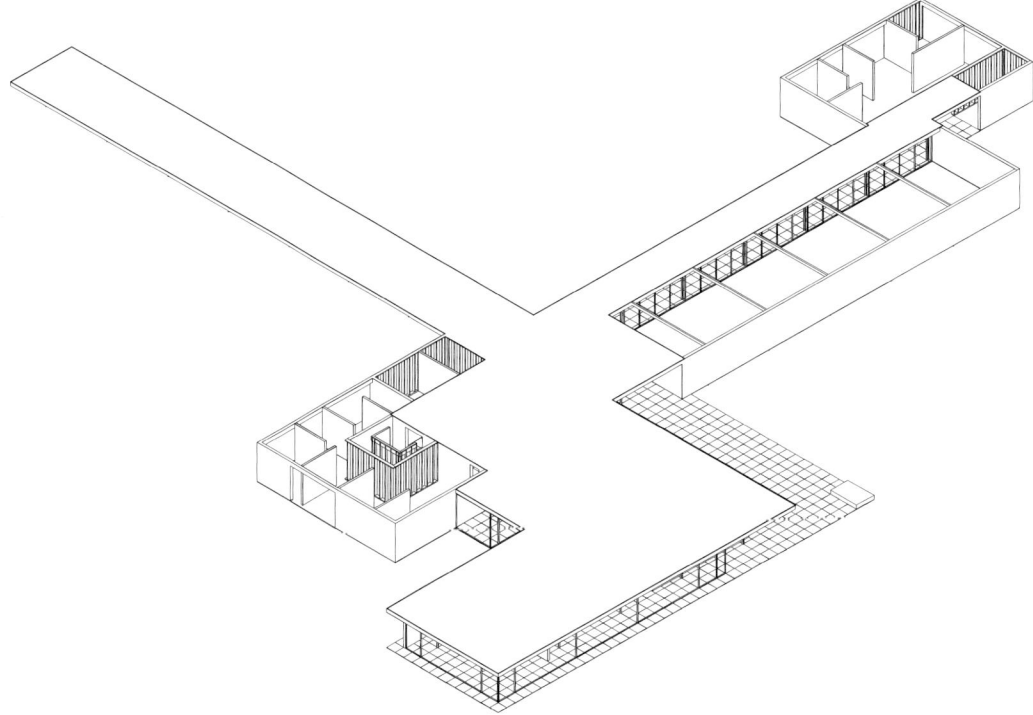

Isometries

Isometrien

South-west Süd-West

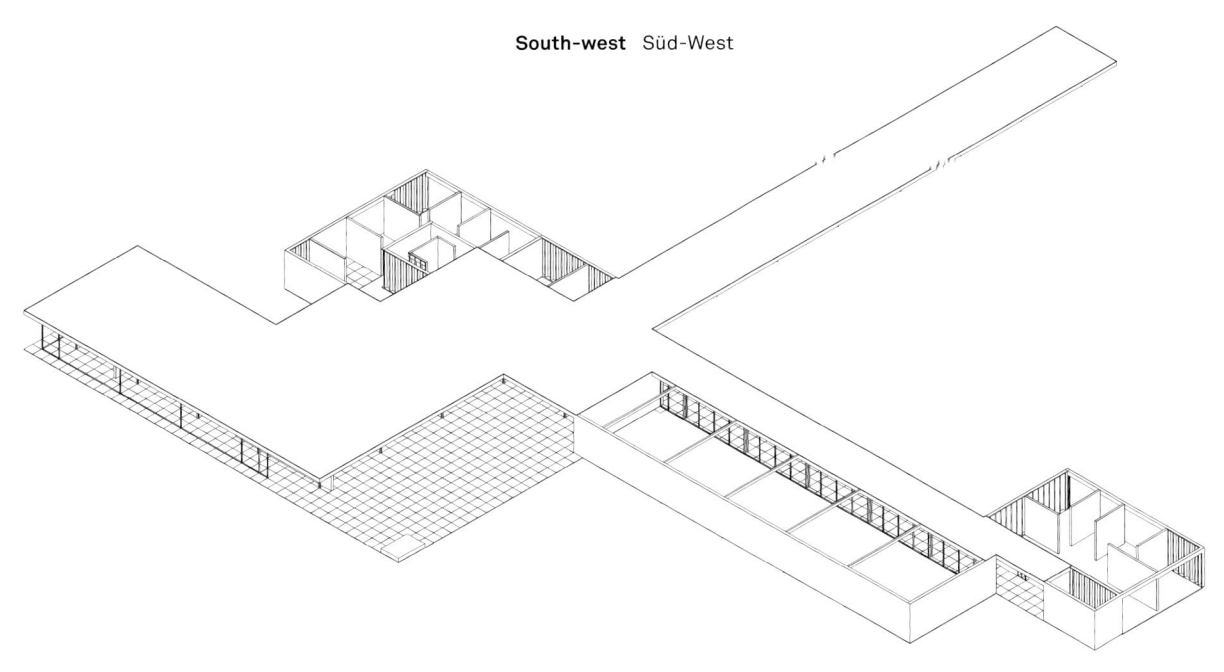

North-east Nord-Ost

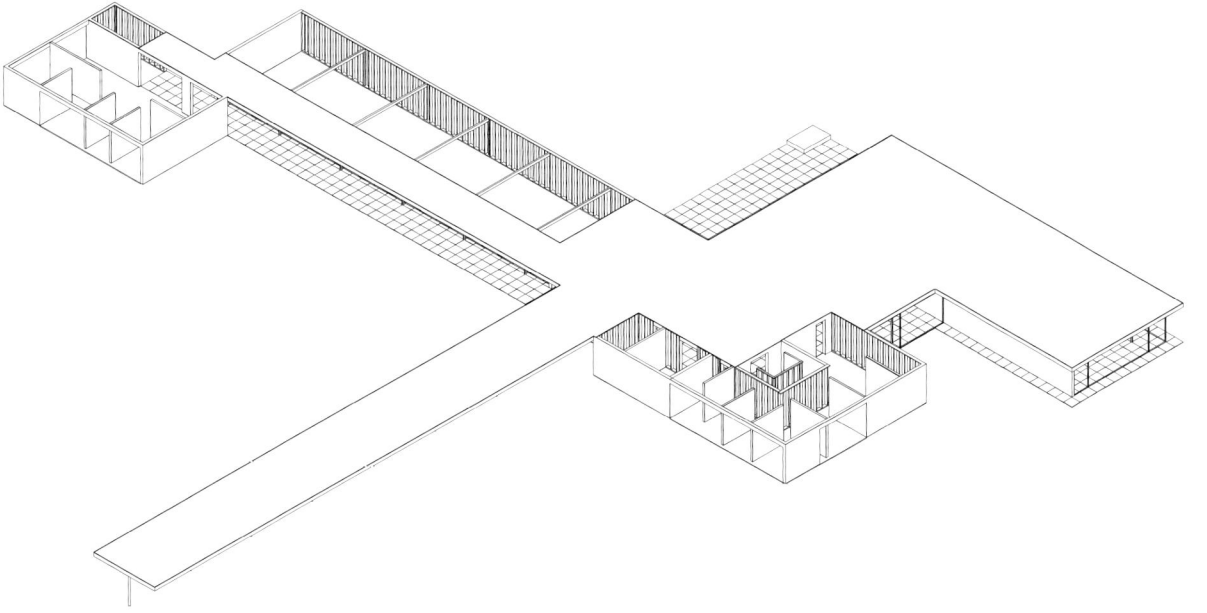

Isometries

Isometrien

1:1, or: The Chasm of the Colon

Reinhard Wendler

When it comes to conceptual definitions, architecture has adopted the same trend found in the technical and natural sciences: it speaks about models in terms of success. If we define a model as a representation (as we often hear natural scientists, engineers, and philosophers of science do), then we are talking about something that has succeeded. By the reasoning of many model-theory definitions, if a model is not a representation then it is no model. In this, at least, they follow the same line of thought as Alfred Tarski's mathematical definition of a model.[1] But even when we speak of models as archetypes, as is often the case when it comes to planning, the focus is on the aspect of success and accomplishment. Something similar applies to models that are used in the search for a solution—i.e. that are intermediate stages and not final results. Friedrich Kaulbach, for instance, writes that such models have the function of "making room for artistic experimentation."[2] This definition, too, is articulated in the language of success that has effectively set the tone for attempts at conceptual definitions for various types of models.

If we take a closer look at specific models and modeling processes in the history of architecture, technology, and the natural sciences, we encounter a remarkably different picture. It becomes clear that a model's

[1] Alfred Tarski, "Über den Begriff der logischen Folgerung", in: *Actes du congrès international de philosophie scientifique*, Heft VII: Logique, Paris, 1935, pp. 1–11.
[2] Friedrich Kaulbach, "Modell", in: Joachim Ritter, Karlfried Gründer (Hg.), *Historisches Wörterbuch der Philosophie,* Band 6, Basel, 1984, columns 45–47, here column 45.

1:1 oder der Abgrund des Doppelpunkts

Reinhard Wendler

Bei Begriffsbestimmungen hat es sich in der Architektur ebenso wie in den Technik- und Naturwissenschaften eingebürgert, über Modelle im Tonfall des Erfolgs zu sprechen. Definiert man das Modell, wie dies vielfach von Naturwissenschaftlern, Ingenieuren und Wissenschaftstheoretikern zu hören ist, als eine Repräsentation, dann spricht man davon, dass hier etwas gelungen ist. Ist das Modell keine Repräsentation, dann ist es auch kein Modell, so schlussfolgern viele modelltheoretische Bestimmungen und folgen darin zumindest im Denkstil der mathematischen Definition des Modells von Alfred Tarski.[1] Aber auch wenn man vom Modell als Vorbild spricht, wie dies in Planungszusammenhängen vielfach üblich ist, fokussiert man auf den Aspekt des Erfolgs und des Gelingens. Ähnliches gilt für Modelle, die bei der Suche nach einer Lösung oder Antwort verwendet werden, also als Durchgangsstadien und nicht als Resultate auftreten. Beispielsweise schreibt Friedrich Kaulbach solchen Modellen die Funktion des „Raumgebens für künstlerisches Experimentieren"[2] zu. Auch diese Bestimmung stellt den Erfolg in den Vordergrund und ist daher ebenfalls in jenem Tonfall des Erfolgs gehalten, der sozusagen zum Tenor der begrifflichen Bestimmungsversuche ganz verschiedener Modelltypen geworden ist.

1 Alfred Tarski, „Über den Begriff der logischen Folgerung", in: *Actes du congrès international de philosophie scientifique*, Heft VII: Logique, Paris 1935, S. 1–11.
2 Friedrich Kaulbach, „Modell", in: Joachim Ritter, Karlfried Gründer (Hg.), *Historisches Wörterbuch der Philosophie*, Band 6, Basel 1984, Sp. 45–47, hier Sp. 45.

success is just a small part of a much more complex process. This gaping chasm between conceptual definition and cultural practice forms the subject of this essay. It is rarely or never addressed in the model's conceptual definitions, but we do find it in other contexts, especially in other media.

One example is Man Ray's photographs of mathematical models, made from 1934 to 1936 at the Institut Henri Poincaré in Paris. One of these photographs shows a mathematical model whose lighting and chosen angle make it look like an African mask.[3] In the photograph, the surface model—which has been optimized with a view to its didactic success—does not act as an intelligible spatial-haptic transmission of an abstract object, but as the ritual object of a foreign culture.

The ambiguity imposed by the camera is nevertheless much more closely related to the mathematical model than one might assume at first glance. It refers, in an aesthetically precise manner, to the trivial fact (in mathematics, anyway) that a model such as this produces a kind of internal contradiction; the suggestion or expectation that it describes a mathematical structure cannot be brought into harmony with the fact that, in all important aspects, it is of a different category than this structure. For all intents and purposes, the surface model overcomes the insurmountable chasm that separates the object from the mathematical structure. The ambivalence that comes to light in Man Ray's mathematical mask shows in its own way that, with the definition of such models, the tone of success and accomplishment hides something important.

In his *Notes on the Cinematographer*, the director Robert Bresson outlined a kind of subcutaneously related understanding of the model. For instance, he writes: "Models. Capable of eluding their own vigilance, capable of being divinely 'themselves'." Bresson is here speaking about laypeople, who should be preferred over professional actors when making a movie. The formulation "being … 'themselves'"[4] is of central importance here, for it makes clear that Bresson did not see models as representations, as something that merely stands for something else without deserving any attention. Instead, he understands the word "model" as describing the intrinsic value and self-will of an inscrutable opposition. He emphasizes "BEING (models) instead of SEEMING (actors)", and understands working with such models strictly as an adventure with an uncertain outcome.[5]

Like the photographs of Man Ray, *Notes on the Cinematographer* talks about something that—in contrast to familiar concepts of models, and with a view towards the astrophysical metaphor of dark matter—could be called the dark side of models: an omnipresent but in definition strangely hidden dimension of failure, self-will, and the confinement of freedoms, all the way to the "restriction of mental and construction potential."[6] The hypothesis we are aiming to make plausible here is that not only the models of Man Ray and Bresson possess such a dark side, but that all models do—including the model of Mies van der Rohe's Golf Club project that forms the subject of this book.

3 See http://graphicnothing.blogspot.ch/2011/05/12-x-photographs-by-man-ray.html (last accessed June 12, 2014).
4 Robert Bresson, *Notes on the Cinematographer*, transl. Jonathan Griffin, Copenhagen, 1997, p. 77. Thanks to Thomas Macho for the tip.
5 Ibid., p. 14.
6 Horst Bredekamp, "Modelle der Kunst und der Evolution", in: Sonja Ginnow (Hg.), *Modelle des Denkens*. Streitgespräch in der Wissenschaftlichen Sitzung der Versammlung der Berlin-Brandenburgischen Akademie der Wissenschaften am 12. Dezember 2003, Berlin, 2005, pp. 13–20, here p. 16.

Schaut man sich konkrete Modelle und Modellierungsprozesse in der Geschichte der Architektur, der Technik- und Naturwissenschaften näher an, dann zeigt sich ein bemerkenswert anderes Bild. So wird etwa deutlich, dass der Erfolg von Modellen nur einen recht kleinen Teil eines sehr viel komplexeren Vorgangs beschreibt. Diese zwischen den Begriffsbestimmungen und den kulturellen Praktiken klaffende Lücke ist das Thema des vorliegenden Aufsatzes. Sie wird zwar nicht oder kaum in den begrifflichen Bestimmungen des Modells thematisiert, dafür aber in anderen Kontexten, insbesondere in anderen Medien.

Als Beispiel seien die Fotografien von mathematischen Modellen angeführt, die Man Ray zwischen 1934 und 1936 im Pariser Institut Henri Poincaré aufgenommen hat. Eine dieser Fotografien zeigt ein mathematisches Modell, das durch die Beleuchtung und den gewählten Blickwinkel wie eine afrikanische Maske erscheint.[3] Das auf seinen didaktischen Erfolg hin optimierte Flächenmodell wirkt in der Fotografie nicht als die verständliche haptisch-räumliche Übertragung eines abstrakten Gegenstandes, sondern als ein ritueller Gegenstand einer fremden Kultur.[4]

Allerdings ist die mit der Kamera oktroyierte Doppelbödigkeit dem mathematischen Modell viel näher verwandt, als man auf den ersten Blick annehmen würde. Sie verweist in einer ästhetisch präzisen Weise auf den für Mathematiker trivialen Umstand, dass ein Modell wie dieses eine Art inneren Widerspruch erzeugt: Die Suggestion oder Erwartung, es beschreibe eine mathematische Struktur, lässt sich nicht damit in Einklang bringen, dass es sich kategorial in allen wesentlichen Aspekten von dieser unterscheidet. Das Oberflächenmodell überspielt sozusagen den unüberwindlichen Abgrund, der das Objekt von der mathematischen Struktur trennt. Die in Man Rays mathematischer Maske ans Licht tretende Ambivalenz macht auf ihre eigene Weise deutlich, dass der Tonfall des Erfolgs und des Gelingens bei der Definition solcher Modelle einen substanziellen Aspekt ausblendet.

Der Regisseur Robert Bresson hat in seinen *Notizen zum Kinematographen* ein sozusagen subkutan verwandtes Verständnis des Modells umrissen. So notiert er etwa: „Modelle. Imstande, sich ihrer eigenen Wachsamkeit zu entziehen, imstande, erhaben ‚sie selbst' zu sein."[5] Bresson beschreibt hier Laien, die bei der Produktion eines Films gegenüber professionellen Schauspielern vorzuziehen seien. Zentral ist dabei die Formulierung „‚sie selbst' zu sein". Sie macht deutlich, dass Bresson in Modellen eben keine Repräsentationen sieht, nichts, was einfach nur für etwas anderes steht und ansonsten keine Aufmerksamkeit verdient. Stattdessen bezeichnet der Ausdruck Modell für Bresson den Eigenwert und Eigensinn eines undurchschaubaren Gegenübers. „SEIN (Modelle) anstatt SCHEINEN (Schauspieler)", betont er und versteht die Arbeit mit solchen Modellen stringent als Abenteuer mit ungewissem Ausgang.[6]

Die *Notizen zum Kinematographen* erzählen ebenso wie die Fotografien von Man Ray von etwas, das man in Abgrenzung zu den vertrauten Modellbegriffen und in Anlehnung an die astrophysikalische Metapher der dunklen Materie als die dunkle Seite der Modelle bezeichnen könnte: eine allgegenwärtige, aber in den Definitionen seltsam ausgeblendete Dimen-

3 siehe http://graphicnothing.blogspot.ch/2011/05/12-x-photographs-by-man-ray.html (zuletzt aufgerufen am 15.10.2014)
4 Mit „Gegenstand" ist im gesamten Text nicht „Objekt" gemeint, sondern „Gegenstand der Bezugnahme".
5 Robert Bresson, *Notizen zum Kinematographen*, übers. von Andrea Spingler und Robert Fischer, Berlin 2007, S. 64. Dank an Thomas Macho für den Hinweis.
6 Bresson 2007, S. 16.
7 Horst Bredekamp, „Modelle der Kunst und der Evolution", in: Sonja Ginnow (Hg.), *Modelle des Denkens*, Streitgespräch in der Wissenschaftlichen Sitzung der Versammlung der Berlin-Brandenburgischen Akademie der Wissenschaften am 12. Dezember 2003, Berlin 2005, S. 13–20, hier S. 16.

One central aspect of the dark side of the model is the surprising complexity of the at first glance unsuspicious transformation of scale. In the 1980s, György Kepes came up with the idea that the phenomenon of scale could be described as an interdependency of continuity and discontinuity.[7] As one example, he gives reduced-scale models of airplanes that are subjected to a series of tests in the wind tunnel. For the plane's aerodynamic optimization, the tipping point between a laminar and turbulent airflow occurs at different times depending on whether we are observing a small-scale model in a wind tunnel or a wing in flight.

These phenomena are called scale effects, and a whole range of measures exists for their abatement. They occur not only in aerodynamics, but for scale models in general, and in almost every case involve enlargements or miniaturizations. Paul Valéry described the essentially tectonic causes of such phenomena as follows: "Everything changes with size. … If one quality of the thing increases according to arithmetical ratio, the others increase otherwise."[8] The partially unpredictable phenomena that arise during scaling are caused by the fact that the differently scaled qualities are interrelated and influence one another.

Considered by itself, this phenomenon is neither fundamentally positive nor negative, but it is assessed differently in different contexts. Where in aerodynamics and other technical fields scale effects are understood as a barrier to knowledge that must be corrected, in poetic and artistic contexts they are frequently viewed as a medium of design and artistic expression. Susan Stewart here singles out one possible interdependency of continuity and discontinuity in literature: "A reduction in dimensions does not produce a corresponding reduction in significance."[9] A reduction in size may even increase an object's significance, so that we must count with shifts in the opposite direction, as John Mack holds: "[T]he reduction in scale is not necessarily a reduction in significance. In fact, it can imply the very opposite."[10] Julian Heynen's essay in this publication presents several examples for which these and similar scale effects were not fought but were put to fruitful use. With works of art such as these, we see that scale effects are just as ambivalent as models. They, too, possess a light and a dark side. Scale models bring these two more or less aporetic fields together, resulting in (according to one's point of view) either an unclear set of problems or an immense range of possibilities.

The 1:1 model of the Krefeld Golf Club is also subject to this ambivalence—and not because it is to be of the same scale as its object of reference. The formula suggests that we understand the number one on the left as representative of the design for the Krefeld Golf Club's clubhouse on which Mies van der Rohe worked in 1930. The right-hand number one stands for the 1:1 model, and the colon represents the ratio between the model and the building that Mies van der Rohe would have built under more auspicious circumstances. Thus the simple formula of 1:1 places heterogeneous as well as complex entities into a suspiciously simple relation—all the more so since, technically speak-

7 Undated interview, Archives MIT Program in Art, Culture and Technology, Cambridge, Massachusetts, I, No. 91.
8 Paul Valéry, "Eupalinos, or: The Architect" (1923), in: *The Collected Works of Paul Valéry: Dialogues*, transl. W. M. Stewart, Princeton University Press, 1971, p. 139.
9 Susan Stewart, *On Longing. Narratives of the Miniature, the Gigantic, the Souvenir, the Collection*, Durham, London, 1993, p. 43.
10 John Mack, *The Art of Small Things*, Harvard, 2007, p. 71.

sion des Scheiterns, des Eigensinns und der Einschränkung von Freiheiten bis hin zur „Entkopplung der Denk- und Konstruktionspotentiale".[7] Die hier plausibel zu machende Hypothese lautet, dass nicht nur die Modelle Man Rays und Bressons eine solche dunkle Seite haben, sondern letztlich alle Modelle – und damit auch jenes von Mies van der Rohes Golfclub Projekt, dem Gegenstand des vorliegenden Buches.

Ein zentraler Aspekt der dunklen Seite der Modelle ist die überraschende Komplexität der auf den ersten Blick unverdächtigen Transformation der Skalierung. György Kepes hat in den 1980er-Jahren den Gedanken ins Spiel gebracht, dass das Phänomen der Skalierung als eine Verflechtung von Kontinuität und Diskontinuität beschrieben werden könne.[8] Eines seiner Beispiele hierfür sind verkleinerte Modelle von Flugzeugen, die im Windkanal einer Reihe von Tests unterzogen werden. Der für aerodynamische Optimierungen wichtige Umschlagspunkt von einer laminaren in eine turbulente Strömung tritt an unterschiedlichen Stellen auf, je nachdem ob man ein verkleinertes Modell im Windkanal oder einen Flügel während des Fluges betrachtet.

Diese Phänomene werden Skalierungseffekte genannt und durch einen ganzen Katalog von Maßnahmen bekämpft. Sie treten nicht nur in der Aerodynamik auf, sondern im Bereich der Skalenmodelle im Allgemeinen und überhaupt nahezu überall dort, wo Vergrößerungen oder Verkleinerungen eine Rolle spielen. Paul Valéry hat die gewissermaßen tektonischen Ursachen solcher Phänomene wie folgt benannt: „Alles ändert sich mit der Größe. [...] Wenn eine bestimmte Eigenschaft des Dinges wächst in arithmetischem Verhältnis, so verschieben sich die anderen in anderer Weise."[9] Die teilweise unvorhersehbaren Phänomene bei der Skalierung werden dadurch verursacht, dass die unterschiedlich skalierenden Eigenschaften miteinander zusammenhängen und sich gegenseitig beeinflussen.

Das Phänomen ist für sich gesehen weder grundsätzlich positiv noch negativ, wird aber in verschiedenen Kontexten unterschiedlich bewertet. Während Skalierungseffekte in der Aerodynamik und in anderen Technikwissenschaften als ein Erkenntnishindernis aufgefasst werden, denen mit Korrekturen begegnet werden muss, werden sie in poetischen und künstlerischen Zusammenhängen vielfach als Medium des Entwurfs und des künstlerischen Ausdrucks verstanden. Susan Stewart hebt eine der möglichen Verschränkungen von Kontinuität und Diskontinuität im literarischen Ausdruck heraus: „A reduction in dimensions does not produce a corresponding reduction in significance."[10] Die Verkleinerung kann die Bedeutung eines Gegenstandes sogar steigern, sodass auch mit gegenläufigen Verschiebungen zu rechnen ist, wie etwa John Mack festhält: „[T]he reduction in scale is not necessarily a reduction in significance. In fact, it can imply the very opposite."[11] Der Aufsatz von Julian Heynen im vorliegenden Band führt einige Beispiele auf, bei denen solche und vergleichbare Skalierungseffekte nicht bekämpft, sondern fruchtbar gemacht wurden. An künstlerischen Arbeiten wie diesen zeigt sich, dass Skalierungseffekte genauso ambivalent sind wie Modelle, auch sie haben sozusagen eine helle und eine dunkle Seite. In Skalenmodellen treffen diese beiden sozusagen aporetischen Felder zusammen, und es ergibt

8 Undatiertes Interview, Archiv des Art, Culture and Technology-Programms am MIT, Cambridge, Massachusetts, I No. 91.
9 Paul Valéry, „Eupalinos oder Der Architekt" (1923), in: *Werke*, Frankfurter Ausgabe in 7 Bänden, Bd. 2: Dialoge und Theater, hg. von Karl Alfred Blüher, Frankfurt am Main 1990, S. 7–85, hier S. 75.
10 Susan Stewart, *On Longing. Narratives of the Miniature, the Gigantic, the Souvenir, the Collection*, Durham, London 1993, S. 43.
11 John Mack, *The Art of Small Things*, Harvard 2007, S. 71.

ing, Mies' design is the result of a reconstruction undertaken in the past two or three years on the basis of an inspection, measurement, and compilation of the surviving documents.[11] In addition, the design and construction works on the model significantly influenced the notion of what Mies van der Rohe may have had in mind in 1930. The 1:1 model is thus not simply a reconstruction of Mies van der Rohe's design, but should also be grouped among the design and research models used in the process of reconstruction. The two ones therefore do not merely describe very different objects, but are interdependent and influence each other. As a result, the formula describes not a static but a complex and dynamic system.

Moreover, the formula 1:1 relates exclusively to the aspect of scale and ignores all other relationships between the model and its reference object. A material object and the reconstruction of an idea are thus placed in what looks like an exceedingly simple and reliable relation. If, however, we contrast this simple formula with the two objects' different categories, we arrive at the hypothesis that the formula does not *describe* this relationship, but *establishes* it. Andres Lepik pointed out this role of the geometric relationship within the context of the architectural models of the Renaissance: "The scale gives the model its relationship to reality and provides for the first association between a project's artistic concept and reality."[12] With the Golf Club model, this relationship is essentially backwards. Here, the scale does not link the design with reality, but relates reality—i.e. the model—with today's idea of the historical design.

In such cases, scale functions as part of a cognitive operation that can be described using Hans Vaihinger's concept of "practical fiction." It places two disparate entities into a relationship of mutual sense-making, in that they mutually fill each other with meaning and presence. The information that we are dealing with a 1:1 model thus has a potential or immediate influence on our perception of various aspects of the building on Krefeld's Egelsberg. Visual presence, tactile quality, sound and smell, proportions, colors, lights and shadow, the interplay of inside and outside, its special thermal situation, its provisional quality in general, its irregular joints, the settling wood, the attention paid to resistance to the elements, and many other aspects all effectively become elusive, restless, because they seem to refer, on the scale of 1:1, to a design from the distant past. Again with Lepik in mind, by being conceived as a model the building is placed onto the "threshold between imagination and reality."

By so ostentatiously undercutting the complexity and dynamism of the design and the building itself—by ignoring them, in fact—tho formula of 1:1 refers to them even more clearly. In this way it becomes clear, as Bresson writes, that the model is truly capable of "eluding [its] own vigilance," of being divinely "itself." Seen in this way, it neither refers merely to something else nor completely avoids its reference function, as could be said of many works of abstract art. Instead, it makes tangible that complex interplay of reference and self-will by which architectural modeling is frequently characterized. And finally, it rebels against the

11 See Lange, in this publication, pp. 64–80.
12 Andres Lepik, "Das Architekturmodell der frühen Renaissance. Die Erfindung eines Mediums", in: Bernd Evers (Hg.), *Architekturmodelle der Renaissance. Die Harmonie des Bauens von Alberti bis Michelangelo*, exh. cat., Munich, New York, 1995, pp. 10–20, here p. 18.
13 Hans Vaihinger, *The Philosophy of 'As If': A System of the Theoretical, Practical and Religious Fictions of Mankind*, Oxon 1924, reprinted Oxon, 2000, p. 48.
14 Lepik 1995, p. 20.

sich, je nach Standpunkt, entweder ein unüberschaubarer Problemkomplex oder ein immenser Möglichkeitsraum.

Das 1:1-Modell des Krefelder Golfclub Projekts ist dieser Ambivalenz ebenfalls unterworfen, nicht obwohl, sondern gerade weil es den gleichen Maßstab wie sein Bezugsgegenstand haben soll. Die Formel legt nahe, die linke Eins als Stellvertreter des Entwurfs zu sehen, an dem Mies van der Rohe 1930 für das Clubhaus des Krefelder Golfclubs gearbeitet hat. Die rechte Eins soll für das 1:1-Modell und der Doppelpunkt schließlich für die Maßstabsentsprechung zwischen dem Modell und dem Bauwerk stehen, das Mies van der Rohe gebaut hätte, wenn die Umstände günstiger gewesen wären. Die sehr einfache Formel 1:1 bringt also ebenso heterogene wie komplexe Entitäten in ein verdächtig einfaches Verhältnis. Und dies umso mehr, als Mies' Entwurf genau genommen das Ergebnis einer Rekonstruktion ist, die in den letzten zwei, drei Jahren aus der Sichtung, Vermessung und Kompilationierung der erhaltenen Dokumente unternommen wurde.[12] Zudem haben die Entwurfs- und Bauarbeiten an dem Modell ihrerseits die Vorstellung davon wesentlich beeinflusst, was Mies van der Rohe 1930 vor dem geistigen Auge gehabt haben könnte. Das 1:1-Modell ist also nicht einfach eine Rekonstruktion von Mies van der Rohes Entwurf, sondern gehört zugleich zu den im Rekonstruktionsprozess verwendeten Entwurfs- oder Forschungsmodellen. Die beiden Einsen bezeichnen also nicht nur sehr unterschiedliche Gegenstände, sondern diese beeinflussen sich zudem gegenseitig, sie befinden sich in einer Wechselbeziehung, sodass die Formel kein einfaches statisches, sondern ein komplexes dynamisches System beschreibt.

Überdies bezieht sich die Formel 1:1 allein auf den Aspekt der Maßstäblichkeit und lässt alle anderen Beziehungen zwischen dem Modell und seinem Bezugsgegenstand außer Acht. Ein materielles Objekt und die Rekonstruktion einer Idee kommen damit in ein scheinbar überaus einfaches und zuverlässiges Verhältnis. Stellt man jedoch gegen diese einfache Formel kontrastierend die kategoriale Unterschiedlichkeit der beiden in Beziehung gesetzten Gegenstände, so wird die Hypothese greifbar, dass die Formel diese Beziehung nicht *konstatiert*, sondern *etabliert*. Auf diese Rolle des geometrischen Verhältnisses hat Andres Lepik in Bezug auf Architekturmodelle der Renaissance verwiesen: „Der Maßstab gibt dem Modell den Wirklichkeitsbezug, er verbindet die künstlerische Vorstellung eines Projekts erstmals konkret mit der Realität."[13] Beim Golfclub-Modell liegt der Fall sozusagen umgekehrt. Hier verbindet der Maßstab nicht den Entwurf mit der Realität, sondern umgekehrt diese, also das Modell, mit der aktuellen Vorstellung von dem historischen Entwurf.

Der Maßstab fungiert in solchen Fällen als Teil einer kognitiven Operation, die man mit Hans Vaihinger als „praktische Fiktion" bezeichnen könnte.[14] Er bringt zwei disparate Entitäten in ein Verhältnis der gegenseitigen Sinnstiftung, indem sie sich wechselseitig mit Bedeutung und Präsenz aufladen. Die Information, dass es sich um ein Modell im Verhältnis 1:1 handelt, wirkt sich so potenziell oder aktuell auf die Wahrnehmung jedes beliebigen Aspekts des Baus auf dem Krefelder Egelsberg aus. Visuelle Präsenz, taktile Qualität, Geruch und Klang, Proportionen, Farben, Licht und Schatten, das Spiel von Innen und Außen, die spezielle

12 Siehe Text von Christiane Lange in diesem Band, S. 65–81.
13 Andres Lepik, „Das Architekturmodell der frühen Renaissance. Die Erfindung eines Mediums", in: Bernd Evers (Hg.), *Architekturmodelle der Renaissance. Die Harmonie des Bauens von Alberti bis Michelangelo*, Ausst.-Kat., München, New York 1995, S. 10–20, hier S. 18.
14 Hans Vaihinger, *Die Philosophie des Als Ob. System der theoretischen, praktischen und religiösen Fiktionen der Menschheit auf Grund eines idealistischen Positivismus*, Leipzig 1927, hier Neudruck Aalen 1986, S. 68.

dominance of classical modernism by pointing to the chasm that separates us from these works and from the spirit from which they originated. In the end, the chasm of the colon thus opens up a range of possibilities by placing the authorities of the past at a distance where they can be modeled.

Translated from the German by Stephan von Pohl

Thermik, überhaupt das Provisorische, die unregelmäßigen Fugen, das arbeitende Holz, die Sorge um die Witterungsbeständigkeit und viele weitere Aspekte, dies alles wird gewissermaßen flüchtig, rastlos, weil nc 1:1 auf den Entwurf einer entfernten Vergangenheit zu verweisen scheint. Nochmals mit Lepik gesprochen, wird der Bau durch diese Auffassung als Modell auf die „Schwelle zwischen Imagination und Realität" gesetzt.[15]

Weil die Formel 1:1 die Komplexität und Dynamik sowohl des Projekts wie auch des Baus so ostentativ unterbietet, ja nachgerade ignoriert, verweist sie auf diese umso deutlicher. Auf diesem Umweg wird im Sinne Bressons deutlich, dass dieses Modell tatsächlich imstande ist, sich seiner „eigenen Wachsamkeit zu entziehen", imstande, erhaben „es selbst" zu sein. So gesehen verweist es weder lediglich auf etwas anderes, noch entzieht es sich vollkommen der Verweisfunktion, wie man dies etwa für viele Werke der abstrakten Kunst sagen könnte. Stattdessen macht es jenes komplexe Zusammenspiel aus Verweis und Eigensinn greifbar, durch das die architektonische Modellierung oftmals charakterisiert ist. Und schließlich rebelliert es gegen die Dominanz der klassischen Moderne, indem es auf den Abgrund verweist, der uns von diesen Werken und dem Geist trennt, aus denen sie entstanden sind. So eröffnet schließlich der Abgrund des Doppelpunkts einen Möglichkeitsraum, weil er die Autoritäten der Vergangenheit in eben jene Distanz bringt, in der sie modellierbar werden.

[15] Lepik 1995, S. 20.

**Joachim Brohm
Mies Model Study
(Golfclub) 2013/14**

Joachim Brohm
Mies Model Study
(Golfclub) 2013/14

139	MMS C X
140–141	MMS BW III
142–143	MMS C III
145	MMS C XII
146	MMS BW V
147	MMS C IV
148–149	MMS C XIII
150–151	MMS BW I

Pictures in the Subjunctive Mood: Models in Contemporary Art

Julian Heynen

A man, a woman, a boy, a girl, hand-in-hand, all naked: a picture of a family. Only one thing jars: despite being correctly proportioned for their different ages, all four figures are the same height. This otherwise entirely realistic sculpture of a *Family Romance*, made by Charles Ray in 1993, is a model; it toys with representation and scale, it stands for something that it resembles but does not replicate. And it shows how open, complex, and idiosyncratic models can be, how far removed from pragmatic prefiguration or an ideal—not only but also, and perhaps particularly, in the visual arts.

At some point in the 1980s art critics started to talk of "model makers." That term lodged somewhere in our memories. It was mainly used of just a few young artists in Düsseldorf. In fact, it wasn't entirely wrong and above all it had the advantage of sounding a little audacious. After all, aren't model makers men who are still children at heart, who find a way of constructing their own dream worlds in miniature? Whatever the case, in practice the term reduced the phenomenon of models in contemporary art to no more than a matter of scale and cleverly applied craft skills. And it was also unfortunate in the sense that it suggested too close a connection between model-making and architecture. Artists as would-be architects? Although there may have been something in that

Bild im Konjunktiv. Modelle in der zeitgenössischen Kunst

Julian Heynen

Ein Mann, eine Frau, ein Junge, ein Mädchen, Hand in Hand, alle nackt: das Bild einer Familie. Nur eines stimmt nicht: Alle vier sind bei altersgemäßen Proportionen gleich groß. Diese äußerst realistische Skulptur mit dem Titel *Family Romance* von Charles Ray aus dem Jahr 1993 ist ein Modell, spielt sie doch mit Repräsentation und Maßstab, steht sie doch für etwas, das zugleich so und nicht so ist. Und zeigt sie doch, wie offen, komplex und eigensinnig Modelle sein können, wie weit entfernt von pragmatischer Vorausschau oder Ideal – nicht nur, aber auch und vielleicht besonders in der bildenden Kunst.

Irgendwann in den 1980er-Jahren sprach man in der Kunstkritik von den „Modellbauern". Das Wort blieb halbwegs im Gedächtnis. Eine Handvoll junger Künstler in Düsseldorf war damals gemeint. Die Kennzeichnung war nicht ganz falsch, hatte aber vor allem den Vorteil, etwas kess zu klingen. Sind Modellbauer nicht diese Kind gebliebenen Männer, die sich ihre Traumwelten en miniature zurechtbasteln? Allerdings reduzierte der Begriff die Frage nach dem Modell in der zeitgenössischen Kunst allzu sehr auf den Maßstab und auf das Basteln. Und er war unglücklich gewählt, weil er das Modelle-Machen allzu eng an die Architektur band. Künstler als verhinderte Architekten? In der Blütezeit postmoderner Architektur lag solch eine Vermutung zwar nahe, griff aber zu kurz. Wenn

during the flowering of postmodern architecture, it was not the whole story. However, if the frame of reference of the "model" is widened to the point where it becomes an all-round umbrella term for diverse artistic strategies, it becomes interchangeable with other magic formulas like "metaphor" or "symbol" and turns into little more than a platitude.

In his acclaimed book *The Savage Mind* (1962), the anthropologist Claude Lévi-Strauss set out his analysis of "mythical thought." Right at the beginning of his study, Lévi-Strauss introduces the notion of the bricoleur making models. Amongst other things, he asks whether the model "may not in fact be the universal type of the work of art." And he points out that the process of reduction—be it in terms of scale or of properties—seems to be connected with a "reversal in the process of understanding." "To understand a real object in its totality we always tend to work from its parts." However, when we encounter a miniature, "knowledge of the whole precedes knowledge of the parts." In addition to this it is also significant that models are constructed, are "man made." "They are therefore not just projections or a passive homologue of the object: they constitute a real experiment with it." This in turn also means that those observing the model are "put in possession of other possible forms of the same work." And Lévi-Strauss concludes that the model ultimately "compensates for the renunciation of sensible dimensions by the acquisition of intelligible dimensions."

These comments by Lévi-Strauss do not, of course, cover every aspect of the role of the model, either in general terms or in the context of art in our own time. However, they do provide some unexpected pointers, in the sense that they lead us straight into the area that interests many present-day artists: that is to say, a realm situated somewhere between pragmatic models on one hand, and on the other hand "mind models," which cover every aspect of intellectual thought, the imagination, and human emotions.

For the artists discussed in the following survey, the model is not necessarily their only strategy and may not even be their preferred sphere of operation. In some cases it plays a prominent part in the artist's repertoire, in others it only occasionally features in their work. Some of them figure in what Paul Robbrecht once called "my world"—an artistic and intellectual milieu that was and still is important to many of his contemporaries—by which he means a particular way of interacting with the world, through one's own works, that informs both his approach and his work as an architect.

Let us start by going right back to the time of the young Mies van der Rohe: in other words, to Russian Constructivism and specifically the flying machine *Letatlin*, which Vladimir Tatlin built around 1930. Our firsthand knowledge of this work is scarce, because it only exists only in one rather neglected version and as later reconstructions. This minimalist device could be described as a 1:1 model and was an entirely serious project: the idea was that a human being would be able to take off and fly using no more than his or her own muscle power. However, by that time aeronautical engineering was already a well-established industry, meaning that Tatlin's design appeared strangely old-fashioned—more like the

man allerdings den Begriff „Modell" ausweitet und zur Allround-Formel künstlerischer Strategien erhebt, droht er austauschbar mit ähnlichen Zauberformeln wie etwa „Metapher" oder „Symbol" und zu einer Dingenweisheit zu werden.

In seinem berühmten Buch *Das wilde Denken* geht es dem Ethnologen Claude Lévi-Strauss in den 1960er-Jahren um eine Analyse des mythischen Denkens. Gleich am Anfang kommt er sowohl auf den Begriff des Bastlers wie auf den des Modells zu sprechen. Ich vereinfache etwas: Er stellt sich die Frage, ob das Modell „nicht immer und überall der Typus des Kunstwerks überhaupt ist". Aus der Verkleinerung – sei es die des Maßstabs oder der Eigenschaften – erwachse eine „Umkehrung des Erkenntnisprozesses". „Wenn wir das wirkliche Objekt in seiner Totalität erkennen wollen, neigen wir immer dazu, von seinen Teilen auszugehen." Umgekehrt „geht im verkleinerten Modell die Erkenntnis des Ganzen der der Teile voraus". Hinzu komme, dass das Modell konstruiert, dass es *man-made* sei. „Es ist also nicht […] eine passive Entsprechung des Objektes: es konstituiert eine wirkliche Erfahrung über das Objekt." Das bedeutet aber auch, dem Betrachter werden damit „andere[r] mögliche[r] Modalitäten des gleichen" Modells eröffnet. Zusammenfassend heißt es schließlich, dass das Modell „den Verzicht auf sinnliche Dimensionen durch den Gewinn intellektueller Dimensionen ausgleicht".

Dieser Verweis auf Lévi-Strauss kann selbstverständlich weder generell noch im Hinblick auf die neuere Kunst allen Rollen des Modells gerecht werden, dafür gibt er aber Anregungen von einer unerwarteten Seite. Er führt nämlich direkt auf jenes Feld, das sich zwischen pragmatischen Modellen einerseits und Denk-, Vorstellungs- und Empfindungsmodellen andererseits für viele Künstler der erweiterten Gegenwart auftut.

Für die in den folgenden Überlegungen erwähnten Künstler ist das Modell nicht unbedingt ihre einzige, mitunter noch nicht einmal ihre bevorzugte Strategie. Bei einigen ist sie unübersehbar, bei anderen spielt das Thema nur dann und wann in ihr Werk hinein. Manche von ihnen figurieren in dem, was Paul Robbrecht einmal „meine Welt" genannt hat. Gemeint hat er damit ein künstlerisches und gedankliches Milieu, das für viele in seiner Generation wichtig war und ist. Dabei geht es um eine Art und Weise, sich mit den eigenen Arbeiten zur Welt zu verhalten, die auch ihn als Architekten betrifft und sein Werk beeinflusst.

Zuerst wendet sich der Blick schlaglichtartig zurück in die Zeit des frühen Mies van der Rohe sozusagen, hier: zum Russischen Konstruktivismus. Man stelle sich den Flugapparat *Letatlin* vor, den Vladimir Tatlin in den Jahren um 1930 gebaut hatte. Unsere Vorstellung von dieser Arbeit ist lückenhaft, denn es hat sich nur eine, stark vernachlässigte Version erhalten, das übrige sind spätere Rekonstruktionen. Man kann dieses minimalistische Gerät ein Modell im Maßstab 1:1 nennen. Es war völlig ernst gemeint: Der einzelne Mensch sollte sich so mit eigener Kraft erheben und fliegen können. Nun gab es damals natürlich schon eine entwickelte Flugzeugindustrie, wohingegen Tatlins Entwurf seltsam altmodisch und so auch traumhaft wirkt. Zudem befinden wir uns in den Anfängen der stalinistischen Diktatur. Der Schwung des revolutionären

stuff of dreams. Furthermore, this was also the time when Stalin was consolidating his dictatorship. The momentum of the revolutionary uprising had noticeably dissipated or even petered out altogether in many areas, not least in artistic circles. And wasn't "around 1930" also the time when many of the hopes and visions of the early days of modernity were in danger of grinding to a halt or even completely foundering? Against this backdrop—and despite its still palpable revolutionary pathos—*Letatlin* looks more like an already melancholic riposte to its maker's own time, like a utopian notion that is proffered despite nagging doubts.

If *Letatlin* is a way of responding to reality through a "modeled" critique in the form of an at least conceptualized alternative, in other areas of Russian Constructivism there are more traditional types of models—as we see in the case of Kasimir Malevich's *Architektons*. These variously stacked and layered models could potentially be constructed, sooner or later—even if their gleaming white surfaces suggest a degree of abstraction that has more to do with the boundless realms of the visionary than with architectural construction in the stricter sense. In fact certain Constructivist sculptures and objects almost seem more like models. To put it rather boldly: does Gerrit Rietveld's famous *Red Blue Chair* have to be a chair? Doesn't it work just as well—possibly better, even—as a sculpture? What if it were suspended from the ceiling? It could then be read as a model for a new approach to life and our environment rather than as merely a chair. Of course this affinity with models in Constructivist objects has something to do with utopian thinking, with far-reaching visions of a New Life and a new role for art (for all the practicality of those objects). The model-like quality of sculptures and objects sustains the notion of the imaginary, not in the sense of illusion and deception, but in the sense of prefiguration, which provides the viewer's imagination with its own room for maneuver.

As we proceed toward the present, let us make just two short stopovers. One at Fluxus, that loose movement that emerged in the 1960s in the West and in the East, that never crossed the threshold to cast-in-stone works, that found its own form of expression in notation, actions, and other ephemera as it focused on communicating both internally and with members of the public. When Tamás St. Turba roughly painted some shapes onto a brick and named it *Czechoslovak Radio 1968*, he created a political model or a model of political communication. And this "radio" only serves as a form of commentary because it does not in fact work. In that conflict situation it is only as a dysfunctional model that it can properly convey certain ideas: rebellion, deceit, impotence.

Our second stopover is closer to the 1980s and involves an artist whose work was highly influential, in Düsseldorf and elsewhere. The artist is Bruce Nauman. His corridors, for instance—simple structures intended for use—are not so much sculptures or environments as "experiments" of some kind. As such it is neither essential nor intentional that they should be perfectly executed. In fact they could be described as three-dimensional sketches that are only developed to the point where the question they are raising can be clearly understood. The same could

Aufbruchs ist bei vielen, nicht zuletzt Künstlern merklich erlahmt oder gar gebrochen. Und ist „um 1930" nicht auch allgemein eine Periode, in der einige Hoffnungen und Visionen der ursprünglichen Moderne festzufahren oder gar umzukippen drohen? *Letatlin* kann vor diesem Hintergrund trotz des noch spürbaren revolutionären Pathos als ein Modell im Sinne eines fast schon melancholischen Gegenentwurfs gesehen werden, als eine ihrer Sache nicht mehr sichere und dennoch vorgebrachte Utopie.

Wenn *Letatlin* eine Form ist, die Realität durch eine modellhafte Kritik in Gestalt einer zumindest gedachten Alternative auszudrücken, finden wir an manch anderen Stellen des Russischen Konstruktivismus Modelle in einem eher traditionellen Sinn. Etwa in den *Architektonen* von Kasimir Malewitsch. Diese vielfach geschichteten und gestaffelten Modelle könnten gebaut werden, früher oder später – auch wenn ihr strahlendes Weiß einen Grad von Abstraktheit suggeriert, der auf das freie Reich des Visionären und nicht auf Baukultur im engeren Sinn deutet. Überhaupt scheinen manche Skulpturen und auch Objekte des Konstruktivismus etwas Modellhaftes zu haben. Etwas ungeschützt gefragt: Muss etwa der berühmte *Rot-Blaue Stuhl* von Gerrit Rietveld überhaupt ein Stuhl sein? Funktioniert er nicht ebenso, wenn nicht sogar besser als Skulptur? Man befestige ihn einmal versuchsweise an der Decke. Er wäre so eher Modell für eine neue Lebens- und Umweltgestaltung als alltägliche Sitzgelegenheit. – Die gewisse Affinität zum Modellhaften im Konstruktivismus hat natürlich etwas mit Utopie zu tun, mit den bei allem Praxisbezug weit vorausgreifenden Visionen eines Neuen Lebens und einer neuen Rolle der Kunst darin. Das Modellhafte hält die Vorstellung des Imaginären wach, nicht im Sinne einer Täuschung, sondern im Sinne einer Vorformulierung, die der Imagination des Betrachters Raum gibt.

Auf dem Weg in die Gegenwart folgen nun zwei kurze Zwischenstopps. Der eine heißt Fluxus, also jene in den 1960er-Jahren sich in West – und Ost – regende lockere Bewegung, die unterhalb der Schwelle des fest gefügten Werkes bleibt, sich in Notaten, Aktionen und anderen Ephemera äußert und so die Kommunikation untereinander und mit dem Publikum in den Mittelpunkt stellt. Wenn Tamás St. Turba einen Ziegelstein durch ein paar grob aufgemalte Formen zum *Tschechoslowakischen Radio 1968* mutieren lässt, dann ist dieses Objekt ein politisches Modell oder ein Modell politischer Kommunikation. Nur weil es nicht funktionstüchtig ist, kann dieses „Radio" einen Kommentar abgeben. Nur als dysfunktionales Modell kann es in einer Konfliktsituation die Dinge auf den Punkt bringen: Revolte, Lüge, Ohnmacht.

Der zweite Zwischenstopp liegt näher bei den 1980er-Jahren und streift einen Künstler, der nicht nur für das Düsseldorfer Umfeld von großer Bedeutung war. Gemeint ist Bruce Nauman. Schon bei seinen zu benutzenden, mit einfachen Mitteln aufgebauten Korridoren handelt es sich weniger um Skulpturen oder Environments als vielmehr um Versuchsanordnungen. Als solche müssen und sollen sie nicht perfekt in ihrer Ausführung sein. Es sind dreidimensionale Skizzen, die nur bis zu dem Punkt ausgearbeitet sind, an dem die jeweilige Fragestellung klar wird. Das gleiche gilt für seine Modelle von unterirdischen Tunneln. Als krude Konstruktionen, die aus Gips oder Gusseisen provisorisch zusammen-

be said of his models of underground tunnels. As crude constructions, provisionally assembled from plaster or cast iron, they transpose (within the confines of the exhibition space) the sensations aroused by the corridors into an imaginary realm of huge architectures. These works are models in less of a technical than a psychological sense. They encourage the viewer to imagine him- or herself in channels circulating underground. Nauman's practice of leaving his works in what looks like an unfinished state, at an experimental stage, rather than perfecting them in the manner of "fine arts," has a fundamental connection with the nature of the model. These works can be characterized as models as a consequence of Nauman's approach to the task, which attaches greater importance to the idea than to the formulation of a sculpture in the traditional sense. At this point it could be relevant to explore the impact of Concept Art, because it played a significant part in the development of the model as a strategy in the work of certain artists. However, this would constitute a rather complex chapter in a different area.

The dominant tendency in Western art around 1980 was, in fact, a more or less vigorous movement directed against Concept Art and Minimal Art, which manifested itself both in experimental Neo-Expressionism and in a reactivation of easel painting. Artists who were working with models, in various forms, were perceived as being only marginally of interest. Things are very different today. And it has to be said that what was happening in architecture at that time, which is now described as postmodern, certainly made an impression on some visual artists—at a stroke it opened new doors for them. Suddenly, or so it seemed, topics such as "picture," "narrative," and "metaphor" had become interesting again and were explored in drawings and built structures alike. The supportive impetus that came from architecture was perfectly symbolized in 1979 in Aldo Rossi's floating *Teatro del Mondo* (a wooden model on a scale of 1:1), which he anchored at the Punta della Dogana in Venice—like a passing architectural image.

Artists such as Ludger Gerdes in Düsseldorf engaged intensively with the conceptual and constructed ideas that were driving architecture at that time, as they had also done in the past. Alternately turning his attention to a conservative re-evaluation of the social role of architecture and to his work on what he himself called a "world-view construction-site," Gerdes developed his own "construction images" in various sizes and also in numerous watercolors as he researched the wide-ranging possibilities of the model and of modes of thought involving models.

Another artist/architect who, since the 1970s, has been preoccupied with the possibilities of architecture as a form of representation for conceptual ideas is the American Siah Armajani. Besides creating models as a homage to particular thinkers or philosophical concepts, he has also produced "grammars" of architectural elements. To a certain extent he uses models in the traditional manner in his preparations for a potential building. However, he has also realized many of these designs and has integrated them into the public arena. The interesting thing is that, even on a scale of 1:1, these constructions still retain something of their character as models and as such differ from comparable, "normal"

gefügt sind, überführen sie – obwohl nur raumgroß – die Erfahrungen mit den Korridoren ins Imaginäre riesiger Architekturen. Es sind Modelle weniger in einem technischen als in einem psychologischen Sinn. Sie verlangen nach der Imagination des Betrachters, sich in die gedachten kreisenden Kanäle unter der Erde hineinzuversetzen. Naumans Prinzip, seine Arbeiten in einer Art Rohzustand, im Stadium der Versuchsanordnung zu belassen und nicht in den Bahnen der „schönen Künste" auszuentwickeln, berührt das Thema Modell in einer grundsätzlichen Art. Der Modellcharakter seiner Arbeiten besteht in einer Haltung zum Werk, die auf die Qualität der jeweiligen Idee setzt und weniger auf die Formulierung einer Plastik im herkömmlichen Sinn. An dieser Stelle wäre die Concept-Art ein eigenes Thema, denn für die Entwicklung des Modells als Strategie bei einigen Künstlern der nachfolgenden Generation hat sie wesentliche Impulse gesetzt. Allerdings wäre dies ein ziemlich komplexes Kapitel in anderem Zusammenhang.

Die dominierende Tendenz der Westkunst um 1980 war indes eine mehr oder weniger heftige Gegenbewegung zu Concept- und Minimal Art, die sich in Spielformen eines Neoexpressionismus und der Reaktivierung des Tafelbildes ausdrückte. Die Künstler, die sich mit dem Modell in der einen oder anderen Form beschäftigten, standen damals eher am Rande der Aufmerksamkeit. Heute sieht das durchaus anders aus. Und nicht zu verschweigen ist, dass das, was sich damals in der Architektur tat und was Postmoderne genannt wurde, durchaus auf manche Künstler Eindruck gemacht hat – im Sinne eines Türaufstoßens. Plötzlich, so schien es, waren dort Themen wie „Bild", „Erzählung" oder „Metapher" wieder interessant und wurden zeichnend und bauend umkreist. Diese Steigbügelfunktion der Architektur wird sehr schön 1979 im schwimmenden *Teatro del Mondo* von Aldo Rossi sinnfällig, wie es als ein hölzernes Modell im Maßstab 1:1 an der Punta della Dogana in Venedig anlegte – ein gleichsam vorüberziehendes Architekturbild.

Nicht nur ein Künstler wie Ludger Gerdes aus der Düsseldorfer Szene hat sich intensiv mit den gedachten und gebauten Ideen, die die Architektur damals – und in der Geschichte – umtrieben, beschäftigt. Changierend zwischen einer wertkonservativen Reevaluierung der sozialen Rolle der Architektur und der Arbeit an einem „Weltbild-Bauplatz" (L. G.) erforschte er in „Bau-Bildern" unterschiedlicher Dimension und in zahlreichen Aquarellen dezidiert die weitgespannten Möglichkeiten des Modells und des Denkens anhand von Modellen.

Ein anderer Künstler/Architekt, der sich seit den 1970er-Jahren mit den Möglichkeiten der Architektur als Darstellungsform für Ideen beschäftigt, ist der Amerikaner Siah Armajani. In Modellen entwirft er nicht nur Gebäude als Hommage an bestimmte Denker oder philosophische Konzepte, sondern auch „Grammatiken" architektonischer Elemente. Das Modell erfüllt bei ihm zum Teil die traditionelle Funktion der Vorbereitung eines möglichen Gebäudes. Es gelingt ihm schließlich auch, zahlreiche dieser Entwürfe auszuführen und in einen öffentlichen Funktionszusammenhang zu stellen. Das Interessante dabei ist, dass diese Konstruktionen auch im Maßstab 1:1 etwas von ihrem Modellcharakter bewahren und sich von vergleichbaren Bauten „normaler" Architekten

architectural structures. If anything they have something of a philosophical air; that is to say, one has a sense that there is a story behind them or an idea that cannot be fulfilled in a function or in aesthetics. It could be seen as a contemporary form of *architecture parlante*—explicative architecture—as it has been known since the late eighteenth century.

The most important and best known artist who has been working with architectural models in the widest sense is Thomas Schütte. Having made models for over thirty years, more recently he has also applied the same principle to structures that are both realized and usable. From the outset his praxis has shifted between two poles: on one hand there are his conceptual, speculative, or emotion-led models, and on the other hand there are his architectural models. When he was invited to participate in the major exhibition *Westkunst* in 1981, he came up with the idea of constructing a ramp from which visitors could survey the entire exhibition zone. However, this proposal had to be rejected since it proved to be unfeasible. Instead, Schütte created a table-sized model of the ramp. Yet this transition into a different scale was not merely a pragmatic fallback position, for it opened up a new realm of "as if," an area where the subjunctive mood comes into play. This in turn created far more open connections between a particular reality (that of a full-size viewing ramp) and an image of that idea (the model). Rather than merely indicating what was "actually" meant and serving as a substitute for that, the model instigates new associations. The question as to how and whether the model should be realized recedes into the background or ceases to figure at all—or almost, since the idea that some of Schütte's models could become a reality subtly increases the drama of the mental images they arouse. The other two models that he showed at *Westkunst* were already the kind of free symbols that could in part be read as commentaries on the new entertainment culture that was starting to pervade large-scale exhibitions of that kind.

In fact Schütte's models from the early 1980s often convey laconic or sarcastic commentaries. That period not only marked the onset of the party-and-design decade, it also saw the last major arms race between East and West. So Schütte created his vision of a bunker as a garden memorial surrounded by poplar trees. Or—making reference to his own métier, which was increasingly buoyed up by society's approval—a very dark anti-museum: that is to say, an incinerator for art. And lastly—anticipating his own end, but also his own career—he produced a monumental gravestone for a certain Thomas Schütte in the form of a pared-back house, which is also seen in another version as a bus shelter. In addition to that, however, there are other models of houses—the studios and artist's houses, for instance—which range from dreamy to despairing. They can be read as deliberations on "the task, the role, and the status of the artist today." At the same time, it seems to be not wholly impossible that these could be realized. Mostly, however, all this plays out—in different scales and off-the-shelf construction materials—on simple tabletops.

Schütte has continued to work with "models" ever since the 1980s. Every so often models interrupt his works focusing on the human figure,

unterscheiden. Sie besitzen einen eher philosophischen Touch, will heißen: Man spürt dahinter eine Story oder eine These, die sich nicht in Funktion oder Ästhetik erfüllt. Eine zeitgenössische Art von *architecture parlante*, eine „sprechende Architektur", wie das seit dem späten 18. Jahrhundert genannt wird.

Der wichtigste und bekannteste Künstler, der das im weitesten Sinn architektonische Modell seit mehr als dreißig Jahren für sich nutzbar macht und darüber hinaus jüngst mit diesem Konzept auch in die gebaute, benutzbare Architektur vorstieß, ist Thomas Schütte. Von Anfang an pendelt seine Praxis zwischen den Polen Gedanken-, Spekulations- oder Emotionsmodell einerseits und Architekturmodell andererseits. Für die große Ausstellung *Westkunst* entwickelte er 1981 die Idee, eine Rampe zu bauen, die einen Überblick über das Gesamtgeschehen der Ausstellung verschaffen sollte. Das Projekt scheiterte damals an der Realisierbarkeit. Ersatzweise entsteht die Rampe als tischgroßes Modell. Dieser Übergang in einen anderen Maßstab ist jedoch nicht nur pragmatischer Notbehelf. Er eröffnet eine Dimension des Als-ob, ein Spielfeld des Konjunktivs sozusagen. Damit werden die Beziehungen zwischen einer bestimmten Realität (der großen Überblicksrampe) und einem Bild dieser Idee (dem Modell) sehr viel offener. Das Bild verweist nicht mehr nur auf etwas „eigentlich" Gemeintes, welches es bloß ersatzweise vertritt, sondern schafft neue Assoziationsfelder. Die Frage, ob und wie das Modell ausgeführt werden sollte oder könnte, rückt in den Hintergrund oder verschwindet fast ganz. Fast, denn die Vorstellung, dass manche von Schüttes Modellen Wirklichkeit werden könnten, erhöht auf subtile Weise die Dramatik der ihnen innewohnenden Gedankenbilder. Die zwei anderen Modelle, die er damals bei *Westkunst* zeigte, sind dann auch bereits solche freien Sinnbilder, die man unter anderem als Kommentare zur damals neuen Unterhaltungskultur solcher Großausstellungen verstehen mag.

Lakonische oder sarkastische Kommentare sind überhaupt in manchen von Schüttes Modellen aus den frühen 1980er-Jahren virulent. Es war ja nicht nur der Aufbruch ins Party- und Design-Jahrzehnt, sondern auch die Zeit des vorerst letzten Wettrüstens zwischen West und Ost. So gibt es etwa die Vision eines Bunkers als Gartendenkmal im Pappelrund. Oder – auf das eigene, immer mehr vom gesellschaftlichen Wohlwollen erfasste Metier bezogen – das ziemlich düstere Gegenbild des Museums als Verbrennungsofen für Kunst. Schließlich, das eigene Ende, aber auch die eigene Karriere vorwegnehmend, der monumentale Grabstein für einen gewissen Thomas Schütte in Form einer Häuschen-Abbreviatur, die in einer anderen Version aber auch als Warteunterstand imaginiert wird. Daneben gibt es jedoch auch die zwischen Traum und Zweifel changierenden Hausmodelle, die Studios und Künstlerhäuser zum Beispiel. Man kann sie als Gedankenspiele zum Thema „Aufgabe, Rolle und Status des Künstlers heute" lesen, und gleichzeitig scheint eine Ausführung zumindest nicht unvorstellbar. All das spielt sich im Wesentlichen jedoch in unterschiedlichen Maßstäben und Baumarkt-Materialien auf einfach konstruierten Tischen ab.

Die Arbeitsform „Modell" hat Schütte auch nach den 1980er-Jahren nicht losgelassen. In seine nun um die menschliche Figur kreisenden

sometimes integrated into public spaces. For all the possibilities raised by the subjunctive mood (in the sense of "unlikely probability") that is often intrinsic to a model, it can also engender a feeling of insufficient commitment. Accordingly Schütte has never given up the idea of taking the step from a model to real architecture. His *Holiday Home T* (2011) has its origins in a not unpolemical model made some years earlier called *Holiday Home for Terrorists* which, having gone through a number of intermediate stages, ultimately became a fully viable structure. But, strictly speaking, this already takes us beyond the remit of the "model," even if a closer examination would soon show that this real architecture still has some model-like features.

The model is also important to another artist who, like Schütte, studied at the Academy of Art in Düsseldorf, namely Reinhard Mucha—and not only in his collaboration with Jürgen Drescher in 1981, when the two artists designed, in all seriousness, a bar for the gallerist Konrad Fischer. In his early, large-scale pieces, Mucha took real objects—such as typical museum accoutrements—and combined these to create mighty, built images, in which the gesture of showing and the process of presentation takes center stage. In other object-like sculptures, found items are put on display and put out of action in elaborately constructed vitrines. In Mucha's hands the vitrine is a model in the sense that it expresses a certain reservation. It functions like a parenthesis, constraining the validity of the exhibit, which is dependent on other, not necessarily visible factors—and these have to be taken into account as conditions that apply to the making of art.

However, for Matt Mullican the model provides not only a welcome means of presenting certain ideas, it is also at the heart of his artistic concept—which, in his case, involves nothing less than attempting to order the entire world. Of course this quest is as fascinating as it is ultimately unachievable. If anything, now in the twentieth/twenty-first centuries, it is an endeavor that seems like an impossible return to the times when the polymath still flourished. This endless, encyclopedic project needs a theoretical framework of sorts: a "thought model." Mullican calls this his "model of a cosmology" and has defined five main categories for his view of the world. These are symbolized by five colors or pictograms. At the same time, he also needs concrete evidence from this world: that is to say, real objects. And this is where the model once again comes into play, as Mullican locates objects in his system or uses sculpture to create a paradigmatic presentation of individual aspects of his program. His work as a whole is, so to speak, a model of his worldview, a model of a way of contemplating the world, rather than merely enduring it.

Because it seems to come from a very different direction, let us also briefly make mention of the work of Manfred Pernice. Pernice is a *bricoleur* of the first order. His entire work is permeated with allusions to architecture, in the form of quotations or simply as "plinths." As a storyteller he is skilled in the arts of reduction and improvisation, as well as in the utilization of leftovers. The crucial factor is that both the form and the contents of his works are fragmentary in nature. And this brings us to

Arbeiten schieben sich dann und wann immer wieder Werkgruppen von Modellen, mitunter integriert in den öffentlichen Außenraum. Der Konjunktiv (im Sinne des Irrealis), der im Modell steckt, kann bei allen Möglichkeiten, die er bietet, natürlich auch ein Gefühl mangelnder Verbindlichkeit entstehen lassen. Insofern hat Schütte die Absicht, vom Modell zur realen Architektur überzugehen, auch nie aufgegeben. Sein *Ferienhaus T* (2011) geht auf ein viele Jahre zuvor entstandenes, nicht unpolemisches Modell mit dem Titel *Ferienhaus für Terroristen* zurück und erreichte über einige Zwischenstadien schließlich seine volle Alltagstauglichkeit. Aber damit sind wir im strengen Sinn schon aus dem Geltungsbereich des Modells heraus, auch wenn eine genauere Betrachtung zeigen würde, dass noch einiges Modellhaftes in dieser Realarchitektur steckt.

Auch für Reinhard Mucha, der wie Schütte an der Düsseldorfer Kunstakademie studierte, hat das Modell seine Bedeutung, und nicht nur in einer gemeinsam mit Jürgen Drescher entstandenen Arbeit von 1981, bei der es um den durchaus ernst gemeinten Entwurf einer Bar für den Galeristen Konrad Fischer geht. In seinen frühen raumgreifenden Arbeiten werden reale Objekte – etwa typische Einrichtungsgegenstände aus einem Museum – zu mächtigen gebauten Bildern zusammengestellt, wobei der Gestus des Zeigens, des Präsentierens selbst in den Vordergrund rückt. In anderen, objekthaften Skulpturen werden reale, gefundene Gegenstände in aufwendig konstruierten Vitrinen aus- und stillgestellt. Bei Mucha ist die Vitrine ein Modell im Sinne des Vorbehalts. Sie funktioniert wie eine Klammer, in der die Geltung des Gezeigten eingeschränkt wird. Das Gezeigte ist von anderen, nicht unbedingt sichtbaren Faktoren abhängig und die müssen als Bedingungen des Kunstmachens berücksichtigt werden.

Für Matt Mullican wiederum ist das Modell nicht nur eine willkommene Möglichkeit bei der Darstellung gewisser Ideen, es ist vielmehr Kern seines künstlerischen Konzeptes. Bei ihm geht es nämlich um nichts weniger als darum, die Welt in ihrer Gänze zu ordnen – ein Unterfangen, das so faszinierend wie unabschließbar ist. Eine Anstrengung zudem, die im 20./21. Jahrhundert wie ein gleichsam unmöglicher Rückgriff auf die Zeiten einer Universalgelehrsamkeit erscheint. Dieses endlose enzyklopädische Projekt braucht einerseits eine Art theoretisches Grundgerüst, eben ein Denkmodell. Er selbst nennt es „Modell einer Kosmologie" und definiert fünf prinzipielle Kategorien, die Welt zu betrachten. Sinnbildlich werden sie in fünf Farben bzw. Piktogrammen. Andererseits braucht es konkrete Belegstücke aus dieser Welt, also reale Objekte. Und hier kommt das Modell erneut zum Zuge, wenn Mullican die Objekte in seinem System lokalisiert bzw. in Skulpturen Einzelaspekte des Programms paradigmatisch vorstellt. Seine Arbeit als Ganze ist sozusagen das Modell einer Weltanschauung, das Modell einer Möglichkeit, die Welt zu betrachten und nicht nur zu erleiden.

Weil sie von einem ganz anderen Ende herzukommen scheint, sei hier kurz auch die Arbeit von Manfred Pernice eingeblendet. Er ist ein *bricoleur*, ein Bastler par excellence. Anspielungen auf Architektonisches ziehen sich als Zitate oder auch nur als Trägerformen durch sein ganzes Werk. Als Geschichtenerzähler kommen ihm die Verkleinerung, die Reste-

another fundamental characteristic of models. All kinds of models work so well specifically because certain things are not included, because their intentional voids act as a spur to the viewer's imagination.

Another American artist, Mike Kelley, only occasionally turned to models, but when he did so, it was in a particularly intelligent manner. Take his birdhouses, for instance, which are in themselves already intentionally anthropomorphic models. In his case they serve to illustrate social norms that acquire their critical force from the effects of minimization or prettifying miniaturization. In his ever-growing Kandors project the "model" has evident links with utopian notions—we have already seen this same connection elsewhere. And Kelley has also used detailed architectural models (in the usual sense) to express his experience of education. His work *Educational Complex* (1995) comprises models of all the educational institutions he attended in his youth. And it is precisely the objective distance of these models that seems to make it possible for him to address a topic so laden with emotional and existential experiences; this process of distancing is not unlike that of Thomas Schütte.

How differently Martin Kippenberger seems to use models. The witty flaneur as a critic of social aesthetics—or so one might think on seeing his *Design for Administration Building for Rest Centre for Mothers in Heilbronn* (1985), consisting of a stack of two pallets, with a section cut out of them. We may think we know his work and that the model seems not to feature importantly in it. However, there is another, more interesting work, where the model figures—but not as a form of miniaturization. This work is the huge installation *The Happy End of Franz Kafka's "Amerika"* (1994). In an area marked out as a playing field, there are countless sets of chair/table/chair, arranged as if for dialogues. The items of furniture are clearly drawn from a wide variety of sources. These groups refer to the mass job interviews that are described at the end of Kafka's unfinished novel. What Kippenberger has created here as an entire scenario could be read as a sociological model, an offbeat diagram, in which the furniture stands for social and economic structures and hierarchies, for inclusion and exclusion, along with the various psychological factors that these imply—all presented as a vast spoof.

In contemporary art the practice of thinking and working in and with models is not confined to individual works. Let us therefore conclude by considering two models of exhibitions. The first is a model-like, as it were ideal reproduction of an exhibition, made by the artist Dominique Gonzalez-Foerster for the sculpture exhibition in Münster in 2007. She filled the meadow by the city moat with a collection of miniature reconstructions of various sculptures from previous outdoor exhibitions in the city. Her models did not point to the future, but to the past; they were souvenirs of a sort. And it was precisely the process of miniaturization, of turning these objects into intimate items able to be easily handled, that caused them to lodge so well in the memories of those who saw them. This work became very popular with the public. The atmospheric nature of the installation raised—but did not answer—the question as to whether it was intended as affirmation or as a critique. A work of art as a miniaturized exhibition of items in other exhibitions: it seems that

verwertung und die Improvisation zupass. Wesentlich ist, dass beides, die Form und der Inhalt, vom Fragment bestimmt ist. Damit kommt ein weiteres grundsätzliches Charakteristikum des Modellhaften zur Sprache. Modelle der unterschiedlichsten Art funktionieren gerade deshalb so gut, weil sie bestimmte Dinge auslassen, weil sie mit gezielt gesetzten Leerstellen der Imagination des Betrachters entgegenkommen.

Ein anderer amerikanischer Künstler, Mike Kelley, hat sich des Modells nur gelegentlich, dann aber sehr intelligent bedient. Etwa wenn er Vogelhäuschen, also in sich schon anthropomorph gedachte Modelle, baut. Bei ihm werden sie zu Illustrationen gesellschaftlicher Normen, die aus der Verkleinerung bzw. Verniedlichung ihre kritische Schubkraft beziehen. In seinem ausufernden *Kandors*-Projekt erscheint die Werkform Modell im Zusammenhang mit Utopie – wir kennen diese Affinität bereits von anderswo. Und schließlich hat Kelley minutiös Architekturmodelle im regulären Sinn eingesetzt, um seiner Erfahrung mit dem System der Erziehung Ausdruck zu verleihen. Die Arbeit *Educational Complex* von 1995 versammelt Modelle der Gebäude all der Erziehungseinrichtungen, die er je besucht hat. Gerade die sachliche Distanziertheit solcher Modelle scheint für ihn die Thematisierung einer so emotional besetzten und existenziellen Erfahrungen möglich zu machen, ein distanzierendes Verfahren, das dem von Thomas Schütte nicht unähnlich ist.

Wie anders scheint dagegen auf den ersten Blick Martin Kippenberger zu verfahren, wenn er Modelle einsetzt. Der wortschnelle Flaneur als Kritiker gesellschaftlicher Ästhetik oder so ähnlich, könnte man meinen, wenn man seinen *Entwurf Verwaltungsgebäude für Müttergenesungswerk in Heilbronn* von 1985 sieht, zwei aufeinandergestapelte Europaletten, aus denen ein Stück herausgeschnitten wurde. So meint man ihn zu kennen, und das Thema Modell scheint hier eher nebensächlich. Interessanter ist allerdings eine andere Arbeit, bei der Modelle im Sinne von Verkleinerungen so gut wie keine Rolle spielen. Es ist die riesige Installation *The Happy End of Franz Kafka's „Amerika"* (1994). Auf einem als Spielfeld markierten Territorium stehen diverse Dialogsituationen in Form von Stuhl-Tisch-Stuhl-Kombinationen beisammen, wobei es sich um Möbel ganz unterschiedlicher Herkunft handelt. Diese Arrangements nehmen Bezug auf das Szenario von massenhaften Bewerbungsgesprächen am Ende von Kafkas Romanfragment. Was hier als Ganzes von Kippenberger entworfen wird, ist so etwas wie ein soziologisches Modell, ein schräges Diagramm, bei dem die Möbel für gesellschaftliche und ökonomische Strukturen und Hierarchien, für Einschluss und Ausschluss samt ihren psychologischen Komponenten stehen – präsentiert als Burleske.

Das Denken und Arbeiten in Modellen in der zeitgenössischen Kunst macht nicht bei einzelnen Werken Halt. Zum Abschluss seien daher zwei Ausstellungsmodelle erwähnt. Das eine ist die modellhafte, gleichsam ideale Reproduktion einer Ausstellung. Es ist der Beitrag der Künstlerin Dominique Gonzalez-Foerster zur Skulpturen-Ausstellung 2007 in Münster. Was sie auf die Wiese am Stadtgraben gesetzt hat, ist ein Sammelsurium von Miniaturnachbauten verschiedener Skulpturen aus den vorhergehenden Open-Air-Ausstellungen in dieser Stadt. Ihre Modelle weisen nicht voraus, sondern zurück; sie sind so etwas wie Souvenirs. Es ist

here the model used for artistic purposes is playing a game of boxes inside boxes.

The second model of an exhibition takes us back to the 1980s and to an intellectual and aesthetic milieu that was not least of considerable importance to some of the artists already mentioned here. The work in question was the *Theatergarten Bestiarium*, which was made by the gallerist, curator, and writer Rüdiger Schöttle in collaboration with a number of other artists. It was a theatrical exhibition of model-like proposals: a landscape of associatively connected designs by artists, all shown together in a single mise-en-scène. The theme was a poetical consideration of the way that works of art and exhibitions might serve as models for society. And this expressly included differences between various elements, as well as other complexities and ambiguities. Not least, this exhibition in the form of a model was a critique of the already emergent rigidification, reduction, and schematization of the all-too fluid art and exhibition business.

In this outline we have touched on models that are variously utopian, political, conceptual, architectural, philosophical, narrative, psychological, skeptical, encyclopedic, sociological, or something else entirely. This little panorama could be continued and could certainly be differently structured. However, it seems wise to adopt a perhaps skeptical view of any attempt to take any overtly systematic approach to the topic of "the model in contemporary art." Which is also why the *Theatergarten Bestiarium* comes at the end of this short survey, since it expressly points to the incomplete and contradictory nature of every model, the chance of a gap into which the uncontrollable images and thoughts of others might plunge. Because here we also have a sense of the great freedom that is inherent in the model—including our own freedom as viewers and users.

Translated from the German by Fiona Elliott

gerade die Miniaturisierung, die Handhabbarmachung, die Intimisierung, die die Objekte in der Erinnerung besonders gut verankert. Die Arbeit war sehr beliebt beim Publikum. Das Atmosphärische der Installation ließ die Frage, ob es sich um Affirmation oder Kritik handelt, in der Schwebe. Ein Kunstwerk als modellhafte Ausstellung anderer Ausstellungen: Hier scheint das künstlerisch eingesetzte Modell als Schachtel in der Schachtel ein Spiel mit sich selbst zu treiben.

Das zweite Ausstellungsmodell führt in die 1980er-Jahre zurück und in ein gedankliches und ästhetisches Umfeld, das nicht zuletzt für einige der hier erwähnten Künstler wichtig war. Es ist der *Theatergarten Bestiarium*, den der Galerist, Kurator und Autor Rüdiger Schöttle zusammen mit einer Reihe von Künstlern geschaffen hat, eine mit theatralischen Mitteln inszenierte Ausstellung von modellförmigen Vorschlägen, eine Landschaft von assoziativ miteinander verbundenen Entwürfen unterschiedlicher Künstler in einer gemeinsamen Mise en Scène. Es geht um ein poetisches Nachdenken darüber, was Kunstwerke und Ausstellungen als Modell für Gesellschaft sein könnten. Und das schließt Differenzen zwischen den einzelnen Elementen, Verwindungen und Ambiguitäten ausdrücklich mit ein. Nicht zuletzt ist diese Ausstellung in der Form des Modells eine Kritik an den schon damals deutlich werdenden Verfestigungen, Verkürzungen und Schematisierungen des allzu flüssig gewordenen Kunst- und Ausstellungsbetriebs.

In dieser Skizze sind künstlerische Vorstellungen von Modell angeklungen, die utopisch, politisch, konzeptuell, architektonisch, philosophisch, narrativ, psychologisch, skeptisch, enzyklopädisch, soziologisch oder anders akzentuiert sind. Das kleine Panorama ließe sich fortsetzen und sicher auch anders gliedern. Eine gewisse Skepsis scheint jedoch gegenüber dem Versuch geboten, das Thema „Modell in der zeitgenössischen Kunst" allzu sehr zu systematisieren. Daher am Ende auch der *Theatergarten Bestiarium*, denn er betont nachdrücklich die Rolle des Unvollständigen und des Widersprüchlichen in jedem Modell, die Chance der Lücke, in die die unkontrollierbaren Bild- und Gedankenimpulse anderer hineinstoßen können. Weil hier etwas von der großen Freiheit des Modells anklingt, nicht zuletzt unserer Freiheit als Betrachter und Benutzer.

Maarten Vanden Abeele Film still from / Filmstill aus *Model 1:1, Krefeld (G)*

Architectural Monument, Cultural Heritage, and the Construction of Memory

Winfried Speitkamp

Before memory, there is the present. It determines identity and the need for identity, classification and categorization, and localization within time and space. It is from here that memory is constructed in order to give identity its origin and foundation: essentially to legitimize it. According to neuroscientists, memory is a constructive process during which our image of the past is constantly being recreated. There is no past other than the one that is present in the present, which is being constantly constructed anew. What does this imply for how we deal with the built-up record and with architectural symbols of the past? This question will be considered in three steps: reconstruction, architectural monument, and cultural heritage.[1]

Reconstruction The history of our approach to historical buildings in the nineteenth and twentieth centuries is also the history of reconstruction. This process produces images of the past and lays traces in the present while, vice versa, opening up pathways to the past. One example of reconstruction is the treatment of cathedrals in the nineteenth century, which were not only stripped down and purified, but also added to—the first and foremost example being Cologne Cathedral. Another example is the chain of castles along the Rhine, almost all of which had

[1] This essay will forego detailed footnotes. The information contained herein refers repeatedly to: Winfried Speitkamp (ed.), *Europäisches Kulturerbe. Bilder, Traditionen, Konfigurationen*, Stuttgart 2013, in particular the introduction and the essays by Gabi Dolff-Bonekämper, Frauke Michler, Eva-Maria Seng, and Gerd Weiß. For a much more detailed version of this essay, complete with documentation of sources, see: Winfried Speitkamp, "Rekonstruktion – Denkmal – Kulturerbe. Über Formen der Konstruktion von Erinnerung," in: *Der Denkmalpfleger als Vermittler. Gerd Weiß zum 65. Geburtstag*, Wiesbaden 2014 (Arbeitshefte des Landesamtes für Denkmalpflege Hessen, 25), pp. 37–48.

Baudenkmal, Kulturerbe und die Konstruktion von Erinnerung

Winfried Speitkamp

Vor der Erinnerung steht die Gegenwart. Sie bestimmt Identität und Identitätsverlangen, Ein- und Zuordnung, Verortung in Raum und Zeit. Von da aus wird Erinnerung konstruiert, um der Identität Herkunft und Basis zu geben, sie gewissermaßen zu legitimieren. Erinnerung ist, so sagen Hirnforscher, ein konstruktiver Prozess, bei dem das Bild der Vergangenheit immer neu geschaffen wird, bei der also Vergangenheit immer neu erschaffen wird. Es gibt keine andere Vergangenheit als diejenige, die in der Gegenwart präsent ist, die immer neu konstruiert wird. Was heißt das für den Umgang mit gebauter Überlieferung und mit architektonischen Zeichen der Vergangenheit? Dies soll in drei Schritten – Rekonstruktion, Baudenkmal, Kulturerbe – erörtert werden.[1]

Rekonstruktion Die Geschichte des Umgangs mit historischer Bausubstanz im 19. und 20. Jahrhundert ist auch eine Geschichte der Rekonstruktionen. Damit wurden Bilder der Vergangenheit erzeugt und Spuren in die Gegenwart gelegt, umgekehrt Wege in die Vergangenheit geöffnet. Zu den Rekonstruktionen zählt der Umgang mit den Domen, die im 19. Jahrhundert nicht nur freigelegt und purifiziert, sondern auch ergänzt wurden, darunter an erster Stelle der Kölner Dom. Dazu zählt aber auch die Kette der Rheinburgen. Fast alle waren nur als Ruinen überkommen.

[1] Der Essay verzichtet auf Detailbelege. Die Ausführungen greifen wiederholt zurück auf: Winfried Speitkamp (Hg.), *Europäisches Kulturerbe. Bilder, Traditionen, Konfigurationen*, Stuttgart 2013, hier besonders auf die Einleitung sowie die Beiträge von Gabi Dolff-Bonekämper, Frauke Michler, Eva-Maria Seng und Gerd Weiß. Eine sehr viel ausführlichere und um Belege ergänzte Fassung dieses Beitrags ist in der Festschrift für Gerd Weiß im September 2014 erschienen (*Der Denkmalpfleger als Vermittler. Gerd Weiß zum 65. Geburtstag*).

been inherited as ruins. Over the course of the nineteenth century, many of these castles were renovated or rebuilt in the spirit of Romantic architecture. Aesthetic interests—which turned the Rhineland into an idyllic model landscape combining nature and culture—were combined with political considerations. With the reconstruction of the Rhine castles, the contested issue between Germany and France (whether the Rhine is Germany's waterway or Germany's border) could be answered symbolically.

One model example of the grand reconstructions of the nineteenth century is the Hohkönigsburg near Sélestat (Schlettstadt) on the edge of the Vosges Mountains in Lower Alsace. The castle, which had been repeatedly destroyed and had fallen into disrepair by the early modern era, was rediscovered in the nineteenth century as a romantic ruin. In 1899 it was given as a present to Germany's Kaiser Wilhelm II, who had the castle rebuilt by architect Bodo Ebhardt in line with its presumably documentable condition from the Late Middle Ages. The result was de facto an idealized version of a late Gothic castle. Its purpose was to act as proof of the German Empire's power, glory, and endurance in the empire's west, just as the similarly restored Marienburg did in the east. After 1918, however, the castle, along with the rest of Alsace, was returned to French ownership. Now it was reinterpreted: the French flag was raised, its historical ties to France accentuated, and its relationship to Alsace and the local population emphasized. Today, the Château du Haut-Kœnigsbourg is a tourist attraction primarily from the French point of view, with no signs of French-German enmity but as part of a landscape of remembrance.

The pavilion that Mies van der Rohe created for the 1929 Barcelona International Exposition represents an entirely different form of restoration. The building was removed in 1930, but its ideas were kept alive in many bungalows and atrium buildings. From 1983 to 1986, the city of Barcelona had the pavilion rebuilt at its original location. It was not a reconstruction, but a copy built in line with monument preservation, and no attempt was made to hide this fact. In the meantime, this rebuilt copy has become a popular building with its own legitimacy, one that—unlike the short-lived original—combines collective identity and memory.

In practice, the reconstruction of buildings in the nineteenth and twentieth centuries was a diverse undertaking, but the functions converged: such buildings were used as storehouses of memory and filled with interpretations and recollections. With the buildings' reconstruction, their history was not yet over; only now did the more or less contentious processes of appropriation begin. The buildings were and are constantly reinterpreted and appropriated by contemporary—and sometimes rival—interests.

Architectural Monument   Few considerations of the history of architectural heritage preservation fail to point out that the definition of architectural monument has steadily expanded. Initially, in the early nineteenth century, the term covered primarily exceptional examples of architecture such as cathedrals and castles, but only if they were in

Im Laufe des 19. Jahrhunderts wurde eine Reihe von ihnen im Sinne der Bauromantik wieder oder neu aufgebaut. Ästhetische Interessen, die aus dem Rheingebiet eine idyllische Musterlandschaft in der Verbindung von Natur und Kultur machten, verbanden sich mit politischen Überlegungen. Die zwischen Deutschland und Frankreich umstrittene Frage, ob der Rhein Deutschlands Strom oder Deutschlands Grenze sei, konnte auch symbolisch mit dem Wiederaufbau der Rheinburgen beantwortet werden.

Musterbeispiel für die großen Rekonstruktionen des 19. Jahrhunderts ist die Hohkönigsburg bei Sélestat (Schlettstadt) im Unterelsass am Rande der Vogesen. Die mehrfach zerstörte und in der Frühneuzeit verfallene Burg wurde als romantische Ruine im 19. Jahrhundert wiederentdeckt; 1899 erhielt der deutsche Kaiser Wilhelm II. sie zum Geschenk. Er ließ die Burg von dem Architekten Bodo Ebhardt gemäß einem vermeintlich belegbaren Zustand des Spätmittelalters wieder aufbauen. De facto handelte es sich um die idealisierte Variante einer spätgotischen Burg. Sie sollte nun im Westen des Reichs wie die gleichermaßen restaurierte Marienburg im Osten von der Macht, Herrlichkeit und Dauer des deutschen Kaiserreichs zeugen. Nach 1918 ging die Hohkönigsburg allerdings mit dem Elsass wieder in französischen Besitz über. Nur wurde sie uminterpretiert: Die französische Fahne wurde aufgezogen, die mit Frankreich verbundene Geschichte betont und der Bezug des elsässischen Landes und der Bevölkerung zur Burg unterstrichen. Heute ist die Hohkönigsburg ein touristischer Anziehungspunkt vor allem aus französischer Perspektive, kein Indiz deutsch-französischer Feindschaft, sondern Teil einer Erinnerungslandschaft.

Eine ganz andere Variante einer Wiederherstellung betrifft den Pavillon, den Mies van der Rohe 1929 für die Weltausstellung in Barcelona geschaffen hatte. 1930 wurde der Pavillon wieder beseitigt, aber die Ideen lebten in vielen Atrium-Häusern und Bungalows fort. 1983 bis 1986 ließ die Stadt Barcelona den Pavillon am ursprünglichen Ort nachbauen. Das war keine Rekonstruktion, sondern ein Nachbau in der Diktion auch der Denkmalpflege, und es wird auch am Ort nicht verheimlicht, dass es sich um einen solchen handelt. Der Nachbau ist mittlerweile populär geworden, er ist zum Bauwerk mit eigener Legitimation geworden, der – anders als das kurzlebige Original – kollektive Identität und Erinnerungen bündelt.

Die Praxis der Wiederherstellung von Bauwerken im 19. und 20. Jahrhundert war vielfältig, doch die Funktionen konvergierten: Derartige Bauwerke wurden als Erinnerungsspeicher genutzt und mit Deutungen und Erinnerungen gefüllt. Mit der Rekonstruktion der Objekte war ihre Geschichte noch nicht beendet, nun begannen erst mehr oder minder strittige Aneignungsprozesse. Die Bauwerke wurden und werden also immer neu von den gegenwärtigen, auch konkurrierenden Interessen her interpretiert und angeeignet.

Baudenkmal Bei Betrachtungen zur Geschichte der Baudenkmalpflege fehlt selten der Hinweis, dass sich der Denkmalbegriff beständig ausgedehnt habe: Zunächst, im frühen 19. Jahrhundert, wurden vor allem herausragende Bauwerke der Baukunst als Denkmäler begriffen, etwa

public ownership. Then, in the late nineteenth century, additional examples of sacral, municipal, and middle-class architecture were added, ranging from churches to town halls. Influenced by the German cultural heritage preservation movement (*Heimatschutzbewegung*), by the end of the nineteenth century even examples of everyday culture were generally considered worth preserving: small farmhouses, fountains, and mills. Starting in the late nineteenth century, the *Heimatbewegung* demanded the preservation not only of buildings, but also of everyday culture and customs, including the revival of traditional folk costumes. The movement also pushed the chronological definition of what was worth preserving closer to the present day. During the first decades of the twentieth century, the definition of cultural and historic monument was further expanded, with entire rows of houses or building complexes being declared architectural monuments. In recent decades, the architecture of the 1950s has also become worthy of preservation. The definition of monument seems almost arbitrary, changeable, expandable, and without limits. Each particular present has redefined its monuments in line with changing and expanding memory interests.

From a legal perspective, the answer to the question of what is a monument is relatively clear and precise, and has not changed in the past two hundred years: a monument is an object whose preservation is in the public interest. This formulation is found in all German heritage preservation laws since the nineteenth century, including—in slightly modified form—in other countries. It justifies the state's intervention and is based on a belief in the general good or the public interest, which supersedes personal property rights. Even the Weimar Constitution of 1919 followed this principle by emphasizing social and cultural elements, and for the first time declaring the social obligation of private property, from which it derived the duty of the state to protect monuments and the landscape. Although the monument preservation article of the 1919 Weimar Constitution was not adopted into the new constitution in 1949, it was included in various regional constitutions, including the 1946 constitution of the state of Hessen.

The belief that in questions of heritage preservation the community comes before the individual has always played a role in preservation debates even though the interpretation of what constitutes the public interest has changed. There have been three dominant schools of interpretation. The *national* approach saw monuments as an expression of national artistic production in general, and of the uniqueness of the nation and national tradition, and it justified their right to preservation on this basis. The *statist* interpretation understood the state to be the bearer of the common will, as a "Cultural State" whose resolute cultural duties must be asserted in the face of individual interests. The monument preservation laws of the various German states in the early twentieth century reflect this statist approach. For the social interpretation, monument preservation was considered *social* policy. The aim was to keep capitalist capriciousness in check while reclaiming quality of life. From this perspective, it was necessary to expand the concept of monument and to include the building's surroundings. Architectural heritage

Kathedralen und Schlösser, aber nur Objekte im öffentlichen Besitz. Dann, im späteren 19. Jahrhundert, kamen auch weitere Dokumente sakraler, städtischer und bürgerlicher Baukultur hinzu, von Kirchen bis zu Rathäusern. Am Ende des 19. Jahrhunderts und unter dem Einfluss der Heimatschutzbewegung wurden auch Zeugnisse der Alltagskultur, etwa kleine Bauernhäuser, Brunnen und Mühlen, als grundsätzlich erhaltenswert angesehen. Die Heimatbewegung forderte seit dem späten 19. Jahrhundert über den Schutz von baulichen Objekten hinaus auch den Schutz von Alltagskultur und sogar Gebräuchen, beispielsweise die Wiederbelebung von Trachten, und sie rückte die Zeitgrenze des Schützenswerten näher an die Gegenwart heran. In den ersten Jahrzehnten des 20. Jahrhunderts wurde der kulturhistorische Denkmalbegriff weiter ausgedehnt, städtische Häuserzeilen oder Gesamtanlagen erhielten nun Denkmalwert. In den letzten Jahrzehnten ist auch die Architektur der 1950er-Jahre denkmalwürdig geworden. Der Denkmalbegriff erscheint fast beliebig, veränderbar, dehnbar und entgrenzt. Die jeweilige Gegenwart definierte ihre Denkmäler neu, gemäß ihren wandelbaren und sich ausweitenden Erinnerungsinteressen.

In juristischer Perspektive ist die Antwort auf die Frage, was ein Denkmal ist, relativ klar und präzise, und sie hat sich seit 200 Jahren nicht verändert: Denkmal ist ein Objekt, dessen Erhaltung im öffentlichen Interesse ist. Diese Formulierung findet sich in allen Denkmalschutzgesetzen seit dem 19. Jahrhundert, auch, in leicht abgewandelter Form, im Ausland. Sie begründet das Eingreifen des Staats. Dahinter steht eine Vorstellung von Gemeinwohl bzw. öffentlichem Interesse, die die reine Eigentumsfreiheit unterläuft. Auch die Weimarer Reichsverfassung von 1919 folgte diesem Ansatz, indem sie sozial- und kulturstaatliche Elemente betonte, erstmals die Sozialpflichtigkeit des Eigentums deklarierte und daraus auch die Pflicht des Staats zum Schutz von Denkmälern und Landschaft ableitete. Der Denkmalschutzartikel der Weimarer Reichsverfassung von 1919 wurde zwar 1949 nicht ins Grundgesetz übernommen, aber in verschiedene Länderverfassungen wie in die hessische von 1946.

Die Vorstellung, dass im Denkmalschutz die Gemeinschaft vor dem Individuum stehe, spielte in den Denkmaldebatten immer wieder eine Rolle, auch wenn die Interpretation, was denn das öffentliche Interesse ausmacht, sich gewandelt hat. Dabei gab es drei dominierende Deutungsrichtungen: Die *nationale* sah im Denkmal den Ausdruck des nationalen Kunstschaffens überhaupt, der Eigenart der Nation wie der nationalen Tradition, und begründete daraus das Schutzrecht. Die *etatistische* Deutung verstand den Staat als Träger des gemeinen Willens und Kulturstaat mit einem dezidierten Kulturauftrag, den es gegen Einzelinteressen durchzusetzen galt. Die Denkmalschutzgesetze der deutschen Einzelstaaten im frühen 20. Jahrhundert spiegeln diesen etatistischen Zugriff. Der *sozialen* Deutung galt Denkmalpflege als Sozialpolitik. Es ging um eine Einhegung kapitalistischer Willkür und die Wiedergewinnung von Lebensqualität. In dieser Perspektive waren die Erweiterung des Denkmalverständnisses und die Aufnahme des Umgebungsschutzes zwingend. Die bauliche Heimat sollte nicht nur in ihren ästhetischen, sondern auch in ihren sozialen Qualitäten geschützt werden. Heimatschutz und Denk-

should be preserved not only in its aesthetic but also in its social qualities. Heritage protection and monument preservation were thus not only an escape from the present into an idealized past, but a modern tool for social regulation.

The socio-political understanding of monument presentation was linked with the idea that monuments belonged to the general public. After 1990, i.e. after the change in system and above all the collapse of the GDR, a new nuance was added to this notion. For buildings (and also for monuments in the narrow sense of the word), the question arose as to what was worth preserving for aesthetic, cultural, or historical reasons, and by contrast what should be removed for political reasons. Behind this question was the debate surrounding countless objects from the communist era, from the Palace of the Republic all the way to monuments of Vladimir Lenin and Ernst Thälmann. The Berlin-based preservationist and cultural historian Gabi Dolff-Bonekämper tried to resolve this conflict by speaking of the conflict value of monuments. The conflict over a monument's preservation or demolition justifies its memory function and demonstrates, through the public's participation, the public interest in the structure. The structures thus concentrate an intricate and contentious history of various social groups whose particular memory interests and identity needs must not be displaced by a hegemonic politics of memory. Here, too, we see the defining criteria of participation and claim to co-ownership. Within this meaning, the material content or artistic value of a monument is less important than accessibility, openness, and the chance to participate on and in the object: to partake in the process of its appropriation, use, and transformation.

Cultural Heritage   As early as the nineteenth century and no later than during the Romantic era, educated Europeans such as Victor Hugo spoke of a common European heritage, one founded in cultural traditions and visibly expressed through architecture. This cultural heritage was essentially the property of all Europeans and had to be preserved for future generations. It was certainly not characterized by homogeneity, but by decentralization and diversity. The nucleus of this European identity was held to consist of idealized commonalities and cultural achievements. These European ideas from nineteenth-century intellectual circles reappeared during the debate surrounding Western traditions after World War II. Nevertheless, to this day the definition of European heritage remains in dispute. As a fixed point in history, Europe is difficult to grasp clearly. It is no coincidence that the Euro banknotes contain pictures of architecture meant to represent various historical eras, but instead of showing any specific buildings, they merely represent stylized architectural forms. In this way, national competition was to be avoided on the notes. What is depicted is a fictitious European cultural heritage. The banknotes recall a common history that never existed while suggesting a denationalization of cultural heritage.

This example underscored the paramount role of architecture in the definition, delimitation, and passing on of European cultural heritage. But is it even clear which buildings possess a specifically European meaning?

malpflege waren insofern nicht bloß Flucht aus der Gegenwart in eine idealisierte Vergangenheit, sondern modernes Mittel der Gesellschaftssteuerung.

Das sozialpolitische Verständnis der Denkmalpflege war verknüpft mit der Vorstellung, dass Denkmäler zum Besitz der Allgemeinheit gehörten. Dem wurde nach 1990, nach den Systembrüchen und dem Sturz vor allem der DDR, eine neue Nuance hinzugefügt. Sowohl bei Bauten wie bei Denkmälern im engen Sinn stellte sich die Frage, was aus ästhetischen, kulturellen oder historischen Gründen bewahrenswert sei, was aus politischen Gründen dagegen beseitigt werden sollte. Hintergrund war die Diskussion über zahlreiche Objekte, die aus der Zeit der DDR stammten, vom Palast der Republik bis zu Lenin- und Thälmann-Denkmälern. Die Berliner Denkmalpflegerin und Kunsthistorikerin Gabi Dolff-Bonekämper versuchte den Konflikt zu lösen, indem sie vom Streitwert der Denkmäler sprach. Erst der Streit über Erhalt oder Zerstörung begründe die Erinnerungsfunktion, er belege qua Partizipation das öffentliche Interesse an den Objekten. In den Objekten bündele sich also eine verschlungene und strittige Geschichte verschiedener sozialer Gruppen, deren jeweilige Erinnerungsinteressen und Identitätsbedürfnisse nicht durch eine hegemoniale Erinnerungspolitik verdrängt werden dürften. Auch hier trat wieder der Anspruch am Mitbesitz, an der Partizipation als Denkmalkriterium hervor. In diesem Sinn kommt es also weniger auf den materiellen Gehalt oder den künstlerischen Wert von Denkmälern an als vielmehr auf die Zugänglichkeit, die Offenheit, die Chance, am und im Objekt mitzuwirken, teilzuhaben an einem Prozess der Aneignung, Nutzung und Veränderung.

<u>Kulturerbe</u> Schon im 19. Jahrhundert, spätestens seit der Romantik, haben gebildete Europäer wie Victor Hugo über ein gemeinsames europäisches Erbe nachgedacht, das in den kulturellen Traditionen liege und in Bauten sichtbar sei. Dieses Kulturerbe sei quasi Besitz aller Europäer und auch für die nachkommenden Generationen zu bewahren. Sein Merkmal sei freilich nicht Homogenität, sondern Dezentralisation und Vielfalt. Als Kern dieser europäischen Identität galten die ideellen Gemeinsamkeiten und kulturellen Leistungen. Diese Europa-Ideen der Bildungswelt des 19. Jahrhunderts tauchen bei der Debatte um abendländische Traditionen nach dem Zweiten Weltkrieg wieder auf. Dennoch ist bis heute strittig, was das europäische Erbe sein könnte. Europa ist als Fixpunkt in der Geschichte kaum sinnfällig zu greifen. Es ist kein Zufall, dass die Eurobanknoten Abbildungen von Bauelementen enthalten, die jeweils für eine Epoche stehen sollen, aber keine konkreten Bauwerke darstellen, sondern nur stilisierte Bauformen. Derart sollte nationale Konkurrenz auf den Noten vermieden werden. Dargestellt wird lediglich ein fiktives europäisches Kulturerbe. Die Banknoten erinnern an eine gemeinsame Geschichte, die es so nie gegeben hat, und suggerieren eine Entnationalisierung des kulturellen Erbes.

Das unterstreicht, welche vorrangige Rolle der Architektur in der Definition, Abgrenzung und Tradierung eines europäischen Kulturerbes zukommt. Aber ist so eindeutig, welche Bauwerke eine spezifisch euro-

What is the relationship between UNESCO's concept of world heritage and the recently created European Heritage Label? The UNESCO World Heritage program, which is divided into cultural and natural heritage, dates back to discussions held at UNESCO as early as 1948. A convention for the protection of cultural and natural sites of international significance went into effect in 1975, and the first twelve world heritage sites were listed in 1978, including Aachen Cathedral and the historic center of Krakow. According to the convention, world heritage sites include monuments, groups of buildings, or other sites that "are of outstanding universal value from the point of view of history, art or science"—i.e. that are within the public interest. Since the 1990s, the World Heritage label has become popular, and is among other things sought out for reasons of tourism and advertising. One frequent criticism is that the World Heritage project has a strongly Eurocentric focus and that political considerations play an important role in sites' inscription onto world heritage lists. Another problem with the label is that the World Heritage Committee interferes in the internal management of cultural heritage and monuments. The world heritage concept represents a claim for co-ownership on the part of the international community that may clash with local interests for the site's use.

By comparison, the European heritage label arose originally from an initiative on the part of various countries, and was initially independent of the EU, which adopted it as an official label in 2011. The EU label is intended for structures that are of exceptional significance on the European level and that are capable of conveying European identity. Thus the aim was to create a "canon" of European monuments. Currently, around seventy objects have been awarded the European label, although these are often buildings or related cultural heritage that are more relevant within the national context. Nationally significant objects that were not considered for the world heritage list were registered as examples of European cultural heritage. For this reason, a criterion was added that the submitted sites must have been of significance for the formation of the European Union and must possess European value.

But what differentiates European heritage from world heritage? Must something be internationally known or at least be of significance for world history in order to be considered world heritage? Do we have a two-tiered system of labeling? Is it even possible to define heritage that is specifically European, i.e. something of special significance for European history alone? Indeed, the concept of cultural heritage is being constantly expanded, with the increased inclusion even of non-material culture, from flamenco to the French culinary arts. As a result, it is becoming increasingly difficult to recognize European cultural heritage as concentrated European memory and to identify tangible expressions of this heritage. Cultural heritage is, after all, defined through participation, through the appropriation of objects and practices.

This brings us back to reconstructions, which represent the clearest and most uncompromising approach to interpreting history. But reconstructions only reveal what is universal to monument care and cultural heritage policy: history is told by visualizing stories and tying them to, or

päische Bedeutung haben? Wie stehen das Konzept des UNESCO-Welterbes und das jüngst geschaffene Europäische Kulturerbe-Siegel in Beziehung? Das Programm des UNESCO-Erbes, aufgeteilt in Kultur- und Naturerbe, geht zurück auf Diskussionen in der UNESCO, die schon 1948 geführt wurden. 1975 wurde eine Konvention zum Schutz von Kultur- und Naturgütern von übernationaler Bedeutung in Kraft gesetzt, 1978 wurden die ersten zwölf Stätten als Welterbestätten eingetragen, vom Aachener Dom bis zur Krakauer Altstadt. Zum Weltkulturerbe zählen gemäß der Konvention Denkmäler, Ensembles oder andere Stätten, die „aus geschichtlichen, künstlerischen oder wissenschaftlichen Gründen von außergewöhnlichem universellem Wert sind" – die also im Blick des öffentlichen Interesses stehen. Das Weltkulturerbe-Label ist seit den 1990er-Jahre populär geworden, angestrebt auch aus Gründen von Fremdenverkehr und Standortwerbung. Vielfach wurde moniert, dass das Welterbe eine stark eurozentrische Ausrichtung habe und bei der Aufnahme in die Welterbelisten politische Erwägungen eine wichtige Rolle spielten. Ein weiteres Problem des Labels besteht darin, dass via Welterbekommission in innere Umgangsweisen mit Kulturerbe und Denkmälern eingegriffen wird. Das Welterbekonzept dokumentiert einen Mitbesitzanspruch der Weltgemeinschaft, der mit lokalen Nutzungsinteressen kollidieren kann.

Das europäische Label dagegen ging ursprünglich auf die Anregung einzelner Staaten zurück und war von der EU zunächst unabhängig, 2011 wurde es dann von der EU als offizielle Auszeichnung übernommen. Mit dem EU-Label sollen diejenigen Bauten ausgezeichnet werden, die auf europäischer Ebene besondere Bedeutung haben und europäische Identität vermitteln können. Es sollte also ein Kanon von Europa-Denkmälern geschaffen werden. Mittlerweile sind rund 70 Objekte mit dem Europa-Label ausgezeichnet. Es handelt sich allerdings oft um Gebäude oder Bezüge, die sich eher in einem nationalen Rahmen erschließen. National bedeutsame Objekte, die nicht als Welterbe infrage kamen, wurden als europäisches Kulturerbe angemeldet. Daher wurde als Kriterium für die auszuwählenden Objekte nachgeschoben, dass sie von Bedeutung für den Aufbau der Europäischen Union waren und einen europäischen Wert aufweisen.

Was aber unterscheidet Europas Erbe vom Welterbe? Muss etwas weltweit bekannt oder zumindest für die Weltgeschichte bedeutend sein, um als Weltkulturerbe zu gelten? Gibt es eine Zwei-Klassen-Etikettierung? Könnte man überhaupt Erbe definieren, das spezifisch europäisch ist, also besonders für die europäische Geschichte, aber nur für sie, Bedeutung hat? Tatsächlich wird auch die Vorstellung vom Kulturerbe immer breiter aufgefächert, auch Immaterielles wird zunehmend einbezogen, vom Flamenco bis zur französischen Kochkunst. Immer schwieriger wird es nun, ein europäisches Kulturerbe als verdichtetes europäisches Gedächtnis zu erkennen und an konkreten Erscheinungen festzumachen. Kulturerbe definiert sich nun durch Partizipation, durch die Aneignung von Praktiken und Objekten.

Das führt zurück zu Rekonstruktionen, die die klarste und kompromissloseste Variante von Geschichtsdeutung darstellen. Rekonstruktionen

reading them into, works of architecture. In so doing, we create not only a view of history but also memory, because monuments appeal to cognitive abilities as well as emotional ties: the objects and memories that have been fed into them establish and consolidate founding myths (e.g. of Europe) and traditions guaranteeing continuity.

    Today's approach to Mies van der Rohe in both Barcelona and Krefeld highlights clearly how architecture connects past and present. It is not the building that stores memory and carries it into the present day. What is more, the memory interests of the present have caused the building to be re-construed either as a copy or a 1:1 model. The question remains whether and how a building can produce a world of emotions and meanings. At the outset, all that is provided is a storehouse of memory ready to be filled. The public interest in the building and its history is not scientifically justified, but must be established in practice at the monument. At the same time, processes of appropriation allow for a constant change in meaning. In other words: history is open, future uses and memories cannot be predicted, and future identity needs will always fill the architectural storehouse of memory anew.

    Translated from the German by Stephan von Pohl

machen aber nur deutlich, was für Denkmalpflege und Kulturerbepolitik allgemein gilt: Geschichte wird erzählt, indem Geschichten visualisiert, an architektonische Werke gebunden bzw. in sie hineingelesen werden. Damit wird nicht nur ein Geschichtsbild, sondern Erinnerung erzeugt, weil Denkmäler nicht nur an die kognitiven Fähigkeiten, sondern an die emotionalen Bindungen appellieren: Über die Objekte und die in sie eingespeisten Erinnerungen werden Gründungsmythen, z. B. von Europa, und Kontinuität garantierende Traditionen gestiftet und verstetigt.

Der heutige Umgang mit Mies van der Rohe in Barcelona und Krefeld erhellt schlaglichtartig, wie Gegenwart und Vergangenheit in Bauwerken verbunden sind. Nicht das Bauwerk hat Erinnerung gespeichert und bis in die Gegenwart getragen. Vielmehr haben Erinnerungsinteressen der Gegenwart dazu geführt, dass ein Bauwerk erneut konstruiert wird, ob als Nachbau oder als 1:1-Modell. Offen bleibt, ob und wie mit dem Bauwerk auch eine Gefühls- und Bedeutungswelt erzeugt werden kann. Zunächst wird lediglich ein Erinnerungsspeicher bereitgestellt, der gefüllt werden kann. Das öffentliche Interesse am Objekt und seiner Geschichte wird jetzt nicht wissenschaftlich begründet, sondern muss durch Praxis am Denkmal hergestellt werden. Aneignungsprozesse am Denkmal ermöglichen aber ständigen Bedeutungswandel. Anders ausgedrückt: Die Geschichte ist offen, künftige Nutzungen und Erinnerungen sind nicht prognostizierbar, künftige Identitätsbedürfnisse werden die architektonischen Erinnerungsspeicher immer neu füllen.

Thomas Florschuetz
Enclosure (GC) 2013/14

Thomas Florschuetz
Enclosure (GC) 2013/14

184–185 Enclosure (GC) 02, 2013/14
186–187 Enclosure (GC) 29, 2013/14
188–189 Enclosure (GC) 04, 2013/14
190–191 Enclosure (GC) 17, 2013/14

It's About the Place

Christiane Lange
in conversation with
Alexander Schwarz
Berlin, May 12, 2014

<u>Christiane Lange</u> You visited the 1:1 model last summer. What impression did it leave on you?

<u>Alexander Schwarz</u>: It's about the place. And it begins with the arrival, with the disbelief on the taxi driver's face when he finds out that he's really supposed to stop at a dirt track that leads into a field.

That's surprising, because a model actually represents something else; and then here, suddenly, it's primarily about the location. It was a wonderful experience to walk along the path through the fields—and it is really just a dirt path—then the grain comes out of the earth and at some point the chrome steel support comes out too, carrying the roof and asserting space. I found that to be a very original and unique experience. It really contradicts the experience of "model" as something representing something else, something more real.

Es geht um den Ort

Christiane Lange
im Gespräch mit
Alexander Schwarz
Berlin, den 12. Mai 2014

<u>Christiane Lange</u> Sie haben das 1:1-Modell letzten Sommer besucht. Welchen Eindruck haben Sie gewonnen?

<u>Alexander Schwarz</u> Es geht um den Ort. Und es beginnt mit dem Ankommen, mit dem Unglauben, den die Adresse beim Taxifahrer hervorruft, er solle tatsächlich an einem Feldweg halten, der dann weiter auf ein Feld führt.

Es ist unerwartet, dass es bei einem Modell, das eigentlich etwas anderes repräsentiert, plötzlich um diese primäre Erfahrung von Ort geht. Es war ein ganz wunderbares Erlebnis, über den Feldweg, der aus Erde ist, zu gehen, dann kommt aus der Erde das Korn, und irgendwann kommt dann aus der Erde die Chromstahlstütze, die ein Dach trägt und einen Raum behauptet. Das war für mich eine ganz originäre Erfahrung, die eigentlich der Erfahrung von Modell, das etwas anderes, Realeres repräsentiert, widerspricht.

It had its own very specific validity as a test arrangement, saying something about the "place," pushing the "place" into another, new sense of space, changing it, so that you see it differently.

The building, which is in fact not a building, borrows—it might be said—the authenticity of the place. It is overlaid by the thesis of this model; this then leads to a very immediate experience that can only be had there, at that place.

CL Do you believe it was important for the act of perceiving the place that Mies planned his design for this concrete location?

AS Well, this was roughly the landscape that was intended and it resonates intuitively with it. I found it interesting that it is in fact really just an unspectacular, normal, German agricultural landscape, which is then suddenly rendered spectacular by the segmentation or reinforcement of the horizon. The undulating horizon against the perfect horizontal: that has a very strong effect. It is less a question of whether that is the actual historically correct location or not; rather, it is about truth. We can feel truth there, although we don't expect it. It is an experienced truth—which is of course an aesthetic experience.

It is the experience of consistency. There is a beautiful sentence from Martin Heidegger: "Übereinstimmung mit dem Seienden gilt seit langem als das Wesen der Wahrheit." (Consistency with the essent has long been the essence of truth.)[1]

But this consistency—wherever the authenticity comes from—is borrowed; the model cannot deliver it. That is simple fact. But that was an essential experience that worked well in its way: a 1:1 model of a building so reduced that it was not a building. We could feel that it wasn't on solid foundations. This made it much more theoretical, much more rootless. The house came into being by occupying the ground, not by changing it; it simply took up its place upon it. The chromed steel supports, growing out of the earth: before that the grain. All of this serves to increase the immediacy of the interconnection of nature and architecture which is inherent to the design.

1 Martin Heidegger, "Der Ursprung des Kunstwerkes" (Vortrag 1935/36), in: *Holzwege*, Frankfurt am Main 1980, p. 21.

Es hatte eine ganz eigene Gültigkeit als Versuchsanordnung, die etwas über „Ort" aussagt – die den „Ort" auf eine andere, neue Räumlichkeit stößt, ihn verändert, sodass man ihn anders sieht.

Das Haus, das ja kein Haus ist, borgt sich sozusagen die Authentizität des Ortes. Diese wird überlagert von der These des Modells, was zu einem sehr unmittelbaren Erlebnis führt, das man eben nur dort vor Ort haben kann.

CL War es in der Wahrnehmung des Ortes wichtig, dass Mies seinen Entwurf für diesen konkreten Ort geplant hatte?

AS Also diese Landschaft war ungefähr gemeint, sie fließt intuitiv mit ein. Ich fand es interessant, dass es sich eigentlich um eine unspektakuläre, normale, deutsche, agrarisch geprägte Landschaft handelt, die dann plötzlich sehr spektakulär wird durch das Ausschneiden oder Verstärken von Horizont. Der gewellte Horizont gegen die perfekte Horizontale. Das wirkte ganz stark. Es geht nicht so sehr um die Frage, ob das der historisch korrekte Standort ist, sondern eher um Wahrheit. Man empfindet dort Wahrheit, was man nicht erwartet hat. Es ist eine empfundene Wahrheit, die ja eine ästhetische Erfahrung ist.

Es ist die Erfahrung von Stimmigkeit. Von Martin Heidegger gibt es einen sehr schönen Satz: „Übereinstimmung mit dem Seienden gilt seit langem als das Wesen der Wahrheit."[1]

Aber diese Übereinstimmung – wo auch immer diese Authentizität herkommt – ist geborgt, das Modell kann das nicht liefern, das ist ganz klar. Aber es war eine wesentliche Erfahrung, die gut funktioniert hat in der Art, in der das 1:1-Hausmodell reduziert war, es kein Haus war. Man konnte spüren, dass es nicht gegründet ist. Dadurch war es viel thesenhafter, viel „leicht-sinniger". Das Haus wurde dadurch, dass es die Erde besetzt, nicht verändert, es setzte sich nur so darauf. Die Chromstahlstützen, die aus der Erde wachsen, davor das Korn, das überhöht noch einmal die Direktheit der Verschränkung von Natur und Architektur, die dem Entwurf innewohnt.

[1] Martin Heidegger, „Der Ursprung des Kunstwerkes", (Vortrag 1935/36). in: *Holzwege*, Frankfurt am Main 1980, S. 21.

CL Some professionals were skeptical beforehand whether the project would work or not. How do you feel about it?

AS When you hear about a project—an accessible model based on a design by Mies—it seems somehow intellectually conclusive, but you have the suspicion that, as a place, it will probably go wrong. There you see a model that is supposed to be a house. This relationship between physical and non-physical has a long way to fall. It can really go wrong.

But as soon as you arrive at the 1:1 model you realize immediately that is going to work. Suddenly it is a place which has something unquestioning about it.

There was a lot of sensitivity involved in implementing it, something I find very admirable. What should be formulated and what should not be formulated ... architecturally. The model also has something cool about it; it was a test arrangement. And it was good that it was temporary.

CL The fact that it was a model provided another kind of reduction, and I believe that this reduction reinforced the architecture.

AS The topic is non-usefulness. All the properties of a building that are useful, except to provide shelter from the rain, were not properties of this building. It was similar to a ruin. When this layer of usefulness vanishes, the naked architectural beauty is revealed. It is interesting that architecture works on both levels unconditionally. Useful and beautiful at the same time. That is not a contradiction. Architecture is just different from art. What is interesting is that you can feel architecture more when it is in a state in which it is either not yet useful or no longer useful. We observe it more as part of nature. That's something that ruins have, that building sites have, and the 1:1 model had it too.

CL The hall with its rows of supports and its wide view into the sloping landscape spreads an atmosphere that draws a Greek temple to mind. What is the classical aspect in Mies' work?

AS Mies' work has a great directness about it which I regard as something classical. It symbolizes nothing but simply is what it is.

CL Einige Fachleute waren im Vorfeld skeptisch, ob das Projekt gelingen würde. Wie ging es Ihnen damit?

AS Wenn man von dem Projekt hört – ein begehbares Modell nach einem Entwurf von Mies, erscheint es intellektuell irgendwie einleuchtend, man vermutet aber, dass es als Ort nicht funktioniert. Da ist ein Modell, das dann doch ein Haus sein soll – dieses Verhältnis von physisch und nicht physisch hat eine große Fallhöhe. Das kann schiefgehen.

Aber bei der Ankunft am 1:1-Modell versteht man sofort, dass es aufgehen wird. Es ist ein Ort, der plötzlich etwas Fragloses hat.

Bei der Umsetzung gab es viel Gespür dafür, was man formuliert und was man nicht formuliert – architektonisch. Wie das gelungen ist, finde ich bewundernswert. Das Modell hatte auch etwas Kühles, es war eine Versuchsanordnung. Und es war gut, dass es temporär war.

CL In dem Modellhaften lag eine Reduzierung, von der ich glaube, dass sie die Architektur verstärkt hat.

AS Das Thema heißt: „Nichtnützlichkeit". Alles Nützliche, das ein Haus hat – außer dass es vor Regen schützt – hatte dieses Haus nicht. Es war einer Ruine ähnlich. Wenn diese Schicht des Nützlichen wegfällt, liegt die architektonische Schönheit blank vor einem. Es ist interessant, dass Architektur auf beiden Ebenen uneingeschränkt funktioniert. Nützlich und schön zugleich – das ist kein Widerspruch. Architektur ist eben anders als Kunst. Aber interessant ist, dass man Architektur in Zuständen, in denen sie noch nicht oder nicht mehr nützlich ist, besser spürt – man betrachtet sie naturhaft. Ruinen haben das an sich, Baustellen ebenso, und so etwas hatte das 1:1-Modell auch.

CL Der „Saal" mit seinen Stützenreihen, der weite Ausblick in die abfallende Landschaft verbreiten eine Atmosphäre, die an griechische Tempelanlagen erinnert. Was ist das Klassische bei Mies?

AS Es gibt bei Mies eine große Direktheit, das erachte ich als etwas Klassisches. Es symbolisiert nichts, sondern es ist, was es ist.

It is not an academic classicism but an endeavour to achieve long-term validity. It also has to do with truth, which at the end of the day comes about almost independently of the author. Seen from this point of view, it is no longer architecture for architects. It has a meaning beyond architecture. It is possible to understand it without knowing anything about Mies. This is also a property of classicism: that you can understand something about it immediately. And if you already know lots about it, you still find it great.

CL Where is the new current interest in Mies' architecture coming from?

AS: Probably there is something in Mies' work that incorporates Modernism, something which Modernism usually doesn't give us. Modernism can be said to be immanent in Mies' work; longings are addressed which are usually left behind by epigone works.

Essentially, we are in fact all modern builders, Postmodernist, or not. That's the way we were brought up. It is pretty difficult to find an architect who doesn't show some degree of influence through Mies.

CL We find that the 1:1 model is difficult to put across to others by means of pictures. Pictures, even good pictures, do not tell that much about the experience that this model allows the visitor access to.

AS I can believe that without question. It is possible to categorize in terms of architecture that looks better in reality than it does on the picture or worse. It's never the same. I'd like to give you one more of those beautiful Heidegger sentences: "Ein Bauwerk, ein griechischer Tempel bildet nichts ab." (A building, a Greek temple, is not an image of anything.)[2] So a building is, together with the place in which it stands, simply original and essential. It escapes the image and the ability to be depicted. I have made the experience that there are essential things in architectural experience which cannot be depicted.

The essence of the happiness that you can feel in some places cannot be depicted. But that is of essential importance to the architecture. It is a

2 Ibid., p. 27.

Es ist kein akademischer Klassizismus, sondern ein Bemühen um langfristige Gültigkeit. Es geht auch um Wahrheit, die am Ende fast unabhängig vom Autor entsteht. Von daher gesehen ist es gar keine Architektenarchitektur mehr. Sie hat eine Bedeutung jenseits von Architektur. Man kann sie verstehen, ohne dass man irgendetwas über Mies weiß. Auch das ist ein Merkmal von Klassik – man kann etwas unmittelbar verstehen.

Und wenn man ganz viel darüber weiß, findet man es auch toll.

CL Woher kommt die erneute Aktualität der Mies'schen Architektur?

AS Wahrscheinlich gibt es in Mies' Werk etwas, das die Moderne inkorporiert, das uns die Moderne aber nicht gibt. In Mies' Werk findet man sozusagen Moderne immanent – hier lassen sich Sehnsüchte adressieren, mit denen uns epigonale moderne Werke zurücklassen.

Im Grunde genommen bauen wir ja modern. Postmoderne hin oder her. Wir sind so erzogen. Es ist ziemlich schwierig, einen Architekten zu finden, der sich nicht auf Mies bezieht.

CL Wir stellen fest, dass das 1:1-Modell mit Bildern schwer zu vermitteln ist. Bilder, auch gute Bilder erzählen wenig von dem Erlebnis, das dieses Modell beim Besucher ausgelöst hat.

AS Das glaube ich sofort. Man kann Architektur einteilen in solche, die besser aussieht als auf dem Bild oder schlechter, das ist nie gleich. Ich will noch einmal einen schönen Heidegger-Satz zitieren: „Ein Bauwerk, ein griechischer Tempel bildet nichts ab."[2] Also ein Bauwerk ist, auch mit dem Ort, an dem es steht, eben originär und wesentlich. Es entzieht sich dem Bild und der Abbildbarkeit. Ich habe die Erfahrung gemacht, dass wesentliche Dinge der Architekturerfahrung nicht abbildbar sind.

Etwas Wesentliches des Glücks, das man an Orten empfinden kann, ist nicht abbildbar. Aber das ist wesentlich für die Architektur. Es ist ein Riesenirrtum, Architektur über Bilder rezipieren zu wollen. Oft heißt es: „Wie sieht's denn aus, machen Sie doch schon mal ein Rendering." Und dann muss man das Bild bauen.

---

2 Heidegger 1980, S. 27.

grave error to receive architecture via pictures. Too often it's a case of, "So how does it look, can you render that for me quickly, please?" Then somebody has to build the picture.

The way air feels that is packaged by the building. That's something that can't be anticipated and certainly can't be made tangible in a picture.

Architectural photography is a medium that exists in its own right, but it is still photography. It is not architecture. It creates an image that is generated during the process of architecture. But it is a fatal error to generate the architecture from the image. Image and architecture exist side by side. But to confuse one with the other has negative consequences.

A drawing is the correct medium with which the promise of the "building" should be formulated. A plan is always a promise. You have to believe me when I say it's going to be great.

CL What remains of the model project, of *Mies 1:1*?

AS *Mies 1:1* could be seen as something similar to a great performance, something you have seen but which was ephemeral. Just like at a concert: those who were actually there had the greatest experience. Documentation is important, but it does not replace the experience. It is something else, something separate.

What remains is the experience that you had when you were there.

Translated from the German by Joseph Given

Wie sich die verpackte Luft anfühlt, die das Gebäude verpackt, kann man nicht antizipieren und schon gar nicht in einem Bild fixieren.

Architekturfotografie ist ein Medium, das es zu Recht gibt, aber es ist Fotografie. Es ist nicht Architektur. Die Fotografie schafft ein Abbild, das durch die Architektur generiert wird. Aber es ist fatal, die Architektur aus dem Abbild zu generieren. Bild und Architektur stehen nebeneinander. Man darf sie auf keinen Fall miteinander verwechseln.

Eine Zeichnung ist das richtige Mittel, um das Versprechen „Bauwerk" zu formulieren. Ein Plan ist immer eine Versprechung: „Sie müssen mir glauben, dass es ganz toll wird."

CL Was bleibt vom Modellprojekt, von *Mies 1:1*?

AS *Mies 1:1* war ähnlich wie eine große Aufführung, die man gesehen hat, es war ephemer. Wie bei einem Konzert hatten diejenigen, die da waren, das größte Erlebnis. Dokumentationen sind wichtig, aber sie ersetzen das Erlebnis nicht, sondern stellen etwas Eigenes dar.

Was bleibt, ist das Erlebnis, das man hatte, als man dort war.

Author Biographies

Joachim Brohm (*1955) lives and works in Leipzig. Since 1993 he has held the post of Professor of Photography at the Hochschule für Grafik there. Since the mid-80s he has had numerous exhibitions and made several contributions to museums and institutions, for example: Museum Folkwang, Essen; SK-Kulturstiftung (SK Cultural Trust), Cologne; Goethe-Institut, London; Kunstverein für die Rheinlande und Westfalen (Arts Society of Rhineland and Westphalia), Düsseldorf; Fotomuseum Winterthur.

Michael Dannenmann (*1959) works as a photographer in Düsseldorf. He studied at the Arts Academy in Stuttgart and at the College of Dortmund from 1992–1997 where he also had a lectureship. Besides photographic works for international magazines, mainly portraits, he is a curator of exhibitions and a jury member for varous competitions.

Thomas Florschuetz (*1957) lives and works in Berlin and Rio de Janeiro. Since the mid-80s he has had numerous exhibitions and made several contributions to museums and institutions; for example, Museum Folkwang in Essen; Berlinische Galerie in Berlin; Museum of Modern Art in New York; Sezon Museum in Tokyo; Tate Gallery Liverpool; Müsczarnok in Budapest; Albertinum in Dresden; the Neue Nationalgalerie; the Hamburger Bahnhof in Berlin and the Kunstmuseum in Bonn.

Julian Heynen (*1951) is a curator and author for contemporary art. Since the 1980s he has curated numerous exhibitions. Since around 1960 he has penned several texts on artists and artistic topics, for example: Bruce Nauman, Thomas Schütte, Katharina Fritsch,

Autorenbiografien

Joachim Brohm (*1955) lebt und arbeitet in Leipzig, wo er seit 1993 an der Hochschule für Grafik eine Professur für Fotografie hat. Zahlreiche Ausstellungen und Beteiligungen seit Mitte der 1980er-Jahre, u.a. im Museum Folkwang, Essen; in der SK-Kulturstiftung, Köln; im Goethe-Institut, London; Kunstverein für die Rheinlande und Westfalen, Düsseldorf; Fotomuseum Winterthur.

Michael Dannenmann (*1959) arbeitet als Fotograf in Düsseldorf. Er studierte an der Kunstakademie Stuttgart und an der Fachhochschule Dortmund, wo er 1992–1997 einen Lehrauftrag hatte. Neben seinen fotografischen Arbeiten für internationale Magazine mit dem Schwerpunkt Porträt, kuratiert er Ausstellungen und ist Jurymitglied für Wettbewerbe.

Thomas Florschuetz (*1957) lebt und arbeitet in Berlin und Rio de Janeiro. Zahlreiche Ausstellungen und Beteiligungen seit Mitte der 1980er-Jahre, u.a. im Museum Folkwang in Essen; in der Berlinischen Galerie in Berlin; im Museum of Modern Art in New York; im Sezon Museum in Tokio; der Tate Gallery Liverpool; der Mücsarnok in Budapest; im Albertinum in Dresden; in der Neuen Nationalgalerie und im Hamburger Bahnhof in Berlin; im Kunstmuseum in Bonn.

Julian Heynen (*1951) ist Kurator und Autor für zeitgenössische Kunst. Seit den 1980er-Jahren zahlreiche Ausstellungen und Texte zu Künstlern und Themen seit etwa 1960, z.B. Bruce Nauman, Thomas Schütte, Katharina Fritsch, Franz West, Andreas Gursky, Miroslaw Balka, Luc Tuymans, Gregor Schneider, Thomas Ruff, Tino Sehgal u. a. Er ist Artistic Director At Large bei der Kunstsammlung NRW in Düsseldorf.

Franz West, Andreas Gursky, Miroslaw Balka, Luc Tuymans, Gregor Schneider, Thomas Ruff, Tino Sehgal and others. He is the Artistic Director at Large for the art collection of North Rhine-Westphalia in Düsseldorf.
Christiane Lange (*1964) is a freelance art historian. For many years she has been publishing groundbreaking research on Mies van der Rohe. Her most recent work is *Ludwig Mies van der Rohe, Architektur für die Seidenindustrie*, 2011.
Johannes Robbrecht (*1977) and Paul Robbrecht (*1950). The architectural practice Robbrecht en Daem architecten was founded by Paul Robbrecht and Hilde Daem in 1975. They have received several awards for their work, including David Chipperfield's invitation to the Architectural Biennal in Venice in 2012. In 2013 Robbrecht en Daem architecten were among the finalists of the "Mies van der Rohe European Architecture Award 2013", the most important European architectural award. Since 2012, their son has been a partner of the practice.
Alexander Schwarz (*1967), an architect, is Design Director and Partner at David Chipperfield Architects in Berlin. After an apprenticeship as a violin maker, he studied architecture in Zürich and in Stuttgart. In his role as Design Director at DCA, he has been responsible for the design of numerous projects and competitions including the following: the Neue Museum and the James-Simon-Galerie on the Museum Island of Berlin, the Museum of Modern Literature in Marbach and the Museum Folkwang in Essen. In addition to this, Alexander has also taken on various academic lectureships.
Winfried Speitkamp (*1958) is Professor for Modern and Recent History at the University of Kassel. In 1994, in Giessen, he completed his postdoctoral thesis on the relationship between the state and the maintenance of memorials in Germany (1871–1933). From 2009–2012 he was director of a BMBF (Ministry for Education and Research) research initiative on European cultural heritage of the twentieth century. He is chair of the Hessischen Landesdenkmalrat (Hessian State Memorial Council) and member of the board of directors of the historical commission of Hesse.
Maarten Vanden Abeele (*1970) works in Brussels as a photographer, filmmaker and artist. His photographs have appeared in international magazines and in books. Particularly his photo series on dance and theater have led to long-standing cooperation with Pina Bausch, the Opéra National de Paris and Jan Fabre, among others. He has documented various projects by Robbrecht en Daem architecten.
Reinhard Wendler (*1972) is an academic at the Art-Historical Institute of Florence. After studying art history, musicology and philosophy in Berlin and Venice, he completed his doctoral thesis on the role of models in processes of works and insight, at the Humboldt University in Berlin, in 2008. Now in 2014, he is an associate fellow in the project *Modelle in der Gestaltung* (models in design and arrangement) at the interdisciplinary laboratory *Bild Wissen Gestaltung* (image, knowledge, design and arrangement) at the Humboldt University in Berlin.

Christiane Lange (*1964) ist freiberufliche Kunsthistorikerin. Zum Werk von Mies van der Rohe publiziert sie seit Jahren grundlegende Forschungsarbeiten. Zuletzt erschien: *Ludwig Mies van der Rohe, Architektur für die Seidenindustrie*, Berlin 2011.
Johannes Robbrecht (*1977) und Paul Robbrecht (*1950). Das Architekturbüro Robbrecht en Daem architecten gründeten Paul Robbrecht und Hilde Daem 1975. Für ihre Arbeiten erhielten sie zahlreiche Auszeichnungen, u.a. wurden sie 2012 von David Chipperfield zur Architekturbiennale in Venedig eingeladen. 2013 ge-hörten Robbrecht en Daem architecten zu den Finalisten des „Mies van der Rohe European Architecture Award 2013", des wichtigsten europäischen Architekturpreises. Ihr Sohn Johannes ist seit 2012 Partner des Büros.
Alexander Schwarz (*1967) ist Architekt und arbeitet als Design Director und Partner bei David Chipperfield Architects in Berlin. Nach einer Ausbildung zum Geigenbauer studierte er Architektur in Zürich und Stuttgart. Als Design Director bei DCA ist er für den Entwurf zahlreicher Projekte und Wettbewerbe verantwortlich, u.a. für das Neue Museum und die James-Simon-Galerie auf der Museumsinsel Berlin, das Literaturmuseum der Moderne in Marbach sowie das Museum Folkwang in Essen. Darüber hinaus hatte er verschiedene akademische Lehraufträge inne.
Winfried Speitkamp (*1958) ist Professor für Neuere und Neueste Geschichte an der Universität Kassel. 1994 habilitierte er sich in Gießen mit einer Arbeit zum Verhältnis von Staat und Denkmalpflege in Deutschland (1871–1933). 2009– 2012 Leiter eines vom BMBF geförderten Forschungsvorhabens zum europäischen Kulturerbe im 20. Jahrhundert. Vorsitzender des Hessischen Landesdenkmalrats und Mitglied des Vorstands der Historischen Kommission für Hessen.
Maarten Vanden Abeele (*1970) arbeitet in Brüssel als Fotograf, Filmemacher und bildender Künstler. Seine Fotografien sind in internationalen Magazinen erschienen und in Büchern veröffentlicht. Vor allem seine Fotoserien zu Tanz und Theater führten zu langjährigen Zusammenarbeiten, u.a. mit Pina Bausch, der Opéra National de Paris und Jan Fabre. Er dokumentierte verschiedene Projekte von Robbrecht en Daem architecten.
Reinhard Wendler (*1972) ist wissenschaftlicher Mitarbeiter am Kunsthistorischen Institut in Florenz. Nach dem Studium der Kunstgeschichte, Musikwissenschaft und Philosophie in Berlin und Venedig promovierte er 2008 über die Rolle der Modelle in Werk- und Erkenntnisprozessen an der Humboldt-Universität in Berlin. 2014 ist er Associate Fellow am Projekt *Modelle in der Gestaltung* am Interdisziplinären Labor Bild Wissen Gestaltung der Humboldt-Universität Berlin.

Chronology of the Program

Compiled by Britta Marzi

Chronologie der Veranstaltungen

Zusammengestellt von Britta Marzi

Lectures and Presentations

3 / 26 / 2013
School of the Art Institute of
Chicago, Sullivan Center, Chicago
Presentation and interview by
Tim Parsons with Christiane Lange

3 / 27 / 2013
Crown Hall, Chicago
Lecture *Mies van der Rohe in Krefeld. An underestimated Period in the Live of the Architect* by Christiane Lange
Cooperation of the Goethe-Institute Chicago, The Chicago Architecture Foundation and the Mies van der Rohe Society

3 / 28 / 2013
Goethe-Institute, Chicago
Film *Mies in Krefeld*

4/ 12/13 / 2013
Museum Haus Lange, Krefeld
Mehr Mies. Modell – Rekonstruktion – Interpretation. 6. Krefelder Architekturtage
(More Mies. Model–Reconstruction–Interpretation)
Lecture "Mies 1:1" by Christiane Lange and Johannes Robbrecht

Vorträge und Präsentationen

26. 3. 2013
School of the Art Institute of Chicago,
Sullivan Center, Chicago, USA
Präsentation und Interview von Christiane Lange mit Tim Parsons

27. 3. 2013
Crown Hall, Chicago, USA
Vortrag *Mies van der Rohe in Krefeld. Eine unterschätzte Periode im Leben des Architekten* von Christiane Lange
Kooperation des Goethe-Instituts Chicago, der Chicago Architecture Foundation und der Mies van der Rohe Society

28. 3. 2013
Goethe-Institut, Chicago, USA
Filmpräsentation *Mies in Krefeld*.

12./13. 4. 2013
Museum Haus Lange, Krefeld
Mehr Mies. Modell – Rekonstruktion – Interpretation. 6. Krefelder Architekturtage Vorträge von Christiane Lange und Johannes Robbrecht

14. 5. 2013
Vlaams Architectuurinstituut,
Antwerpen, Belgien
Vortrag und Diskussion mit Christiane Lange,

5 / 14 / 2013
Vlaams Architectuurinstituut,
Antwerp, Belgium
Lecture and discussion with Christiane Lange, Paul Robbrecht and Prof. Dr. Christoph Grafe
Online: http://www.vai.be/nl/nieuws/lezing-van-paul-robbrecht-en-christiane-lange-gemist-herbeluister-ze-hier

5 / 26 / 2013
Opening *Mies 1:1 The Golf Club Project*
Introduction and lectures by Christiane Lange, Gregor Kathstede, Mayor of the City of Krefeld, Paul Robbrecht, Dr. Wolfgang Melchert

10 / 22 / 2013
Arts Club, Chicago
Lecture by Christiane Lange

10 / 23 / 2013
Graham Foundation, Chicago
Lecture and discussion *The Model as S(t)imulation, Visualization and Prototype* with Christiane Lange, Paul Robbrecht and Julian Heynen, in cooperation with the Goethe-Institute

1 / 16 / 2014
TU Munich, Department of Architecture, *Zukunft und so* (Future and so) lecture by Christiane Lange

2 / 18 / 2014 Architectural Association School of Architecture, London
Lectures and discussion with Christiane Lange, Julian Heynen and Paul Robbrecht, moderation Valentin Bontjes van Beek.
Online: www.aaschool.ac.uk/VIDEO/lecture.php?ID=2382

Academic Program within 1:1 Model

6 / 2 / 2013
Touching Mies
Prof. Dr.-Ing. Winfried Nerdinger,
 NS-Dokumentationszentrum München
Prof. Dr. Wolf Tegethoff, Zentralinstitut für
 Kunstgeschichte, Munich
Paul Robbrecht, Robbrecht en Daem architecten,
 Ghent
Dr. Julian Heynen, Kunstsammlung NRW,
 Düsseldorf
Dr. Miroslav Ambroz, Brünn
Alexander Schwarz, David Chipperfield Architects,
 Berlin
Online: www.lisa.gerda-henkel-stiftung.de
Sponsored by the Gerda-Henkel-Stiftung

Film *Haus Tugendhat* (D 2013)

Paul Robbrecht und Prof. Dr. Christoph Grafe
Online: http://www.vai.be/nl/nieuws/lezing-van-paul-robbrecht-en-christiane-lange-gemist-herbeluister-ze-hier

26. 5. 2013
Eröffnung *Mies 1:1 Das Golfclub Projekt*
Einführung und Vorträge von Christiane Lange, Gregor Kathstede, Oberbürgermeister der Stadt Krefeld, Paul Robbrecht, Dr. Wolfgang Melchert

22. 10. 2013
Arts Club, Chicago, USA
Vortrag von Christiane Lange

23. 10. 2013
Graham Foundation, Chicago, USA
Vorträge und Diskussion *The Model as S(t)imulation, Visualization and Prototype* (Das Modell als Stimulation, Visualisierung und Prototyp) mit Christiane Lange, Paul Robbrecht und Julian Heynen, in Kooperation mit dem Goethe-Institut

16. 1. 2014
TU München, Fachschaft Architektur,
Zukunft und so
Vortrag von Christiane Lange

18. 2. 2014
Architectural Association School of
 Architecture, London, GB
Vorträge und Diskussion mit Christiane Lange, Julian Heynen und Paul Robbrecht, Moderation Valentin Bontjes van Beek
Online: www.aaschool.ac.uk/VIDEO/lecture.php?ID=2382

Wissenschaftliche Veranstaltungen
 im 1:1-Modell

2. 6. 2013
Touching Mies
Prof. Dr.-Ing. Winfried Nerdinger,
 NS-Dokumentationszentrum München
Prof. Dr. Wolf Tegethoff, Zentralinstitut für
 Kunstgeschichte, München
Paul Robbrecht, Robbrecht en Daem architecten,
 Gent
Dr. Julian Heynen, Kunstsammlung NRW,
 Düsseldorf
Dr. Miroslav Ambroz, Brünn
Alexander Schwarz, David Chipperfield Architects,
 Berlin
Online: www.lisa.gerda-henkel-stiftung.de
Gefördert von der Gerda Henkel Stiftung

Filmpräsentation *Haus Tugendhat* (D 2013)

7 / 14 / 2013
Erinnerung und Identität
(Memory and Identity)
Prof. Dr. Winfried Speitkamp, University of Kassel
Wilfried Kuehn, Kuehn Malvezzi Architects, Berlin
Zvi Goldstein, Jerusalem
Prof. Dr. Wolfgang Sonne, TU Dortmund
Prof. Dr. Wolfgang Pehnt, Cologne
Sponsored by the city of Krefeld

Film: Historic film material of the city of Krefeld with explanations by the former director of the town archive Krefeld, Paul-Günter Schulte

9 / 15 / 2013
Das Modell (The Model)
Oliver Elser, Deutsches Architekturmuseum, Frankfurt a. M.
Reinhard Wendler, Zürcher Hochschule der Künste, Zurich
Stefaan Vervoort, University of Ghent, Ghent
Dr. Julian Heynen, Kunstsammlung NRW, Düsseldorf
Dr. Julian Heynen in conversation with Paul Robbrecht and in conversation with Thomas Schütte, Düsseldorf
www.lisa.gerda-henkel-stiftung.de
Sponsored by the Gerda-Henkel-Stiftung

Film: *Mock-Ups in Close-Up* (film collage) by Gabu Heindl and Drehli Robnik, Vienna

Workshops

4 / 21 / 2013
Recycling Mies – Initial workshop for project of the University program. Design students (University of Applied sciences, Krefeld) and architecture students (RWTH Aachen) contrive pavilions from the materials of the 1:1 model, they will use after deconstruction.
Projekt MIK e.V. in cooperation with Prof. Nicolas Beucker, Prof. Dr. Sigrun Prahl, Hochschule Niederrhein, Krefeld, and Prof. Bernadette Heiermann, Anna Weber, RWTH Aachen.

7 / 21 / 2013
Presentation of the team *Recycling Mies* from the University of Applied sciences, Krefeld

7 /21/ 2013
Presentation of the team Arbeitsgruppe *Recycling Mies* from RWTH Aachen in the 1:1 model

6 / 2 / 2013
Baukultur lokal. 1st Workshop. Public participation: citizens, representatives of local building administration, architects, investors and Projekt MIK e.V. discuss perspectives of local building culture and identity of the city.

14. 7. 2013
Erinnerung und Identität
Prof. Dr. Winfried Speitkamp, Universität Kassel
Wilfried Kuehn, Kuehn Malvezzi Architects, Berlin
Zvi Goldstein, Jerusalem
Prof. Dr. Wolfgang Sonne, TU Dortmund
Prof. Dr. Wolfgang Pehnt, Köln
Gefördert von der Stadt Krefeld

Filmpräsentation: Historische Filmaufnahmen von Krefeld mit Erläuterungen des ehemaligen Leiters des Stadtarchivs Krefeld, Paul-Günter Schulte

15. 9. 2013
Das Modell
Oliver Elser, Deutsches Architekturmuseum, Frankfurt a. M.
Reinhard Wendler, Zürcher Hochschule der Künste, Zürich
Stefaan Vervoort, Universität Gent, Gent
Dr. Julian Heynen, Kunstsammlung NRW, Düsseldorf
Dr. Julian Heynen im Gespräch mit Paul Robbrecht und im Gespräch mit Thomas Schütte, Düsseldorf
Online: www.lisa.gerda-henkel-stiftung.de
Gefördert von der Gerda-Henkel-Stiftung.

Filmpräsentation: *Mock-Ups in Close-Up* (Filmcollage) von Gabu Heindl und Drehli Robnik, Wien

Workshops

21. 4. 2013
Recycling Mies – Auftaktworkshop des Hochschulprojekts
Studierende der Fächer Design (Hochschule Niederrhein) und Architektur (RWTH Aachen) entwickeln Pavillons, die aus den Materialien des 1:1-Modells nach dessen Abbau errichtet werden.
Projekt MIK e.V. in Kooperation mit Prof. Nicolas Beucker, Prof. Dr. Sigrun Prahl, Hochschule Niederrhein, Krefeld, und Prof. Bernadette Heiermann, Anna Weber, RWTH Aachen

2. 6. 2013
Baukultur lokal. 1. Workshop
Interessierte Bürger, Vertreter der städtischen Bauverwaltung, Architekten, Investoren und Projekt MIK e.V. diskutieren die Perspektiven lokaler städtischer Baukultur und der Stadtidentität.

2. 7. 2013
Präsentation der Arbeitsgruppe *Recycling Mies* in der Hochschule Niederrhein, Krefeld

14. 7. 2013
Baukultur lokal. 2. Workshop

21. 7. 2013
Präsentation der Arbeitsgruppe *Recycling Mies* der RWTH Aachen im 1:1-Modell

7 / 14 / 2013
Baukultur lokal, 2nd workshop

9/ 19–21 / 2013
Summer academy *Mies meets material – under construction* with students of the Bergische Universität Wuppertal, of FH Aachen and MSA Münster supervised by Prof. Annette Hillebrandt
online: www.fh-muenster.de/fb5/downloads/departments/schemel/mies_workshop.pdf

Mies & Muse, Local cultural events

6/ 20 / 2013   Double concert: Imbroglio and Horst Hansen Trio

6 / 27 / 2013   Reading: Annual finals of *Papp a la Papp*-Poetry slams.

7 / 1 / 2013   Reading: *Ohrenschmaus. Vier Vorleser – Vier Bücher – Vergänglicher Ort!* (Ear drops. Four Readers – Four Books – Fading Place!)

7 / 4 / 2013   Reading: *Die verborgene Ordnung* (The Hidden Order) with Alfred van Cleef as part of the 14. Literarischer Sommer (*Literary Summer*).

7 / 25 / 2013   Concert: *Vue sur les jardins interdits*, Linos Saxophon Quartett

8 / 15 / 2013   Dance performance: *About Skys – Mies van der Rohe. Body – Architecture – City*. Kaiser Antonino and Guest Artists, Duisburg/Tel Aviv

8 / 22 / 2013   Concert: *Mies 1:1 x 2insicht*

8 / 29 / 2013   Concert: *Less is more* phase : : vier

9 / 5 / 2013   Cabaret: *Spass satt* with Volker Diefes and Michael C. Kent (Music)

9 / 19 / 2013   Concert: *Art of Voice goes Mies*. Vokalensemble

9 / 26 / 2013   Concert: Mohammad Reza Mortazavi, Iran

9 / 27–29 / 2013   Installation: Peter Welz, Berlin *Casa Malaparte – Mies [1:1 Golfclub]*

10 / 3 / 2013   Theatre play: *Wir und der Golfclub (UA)* (Us and the Golf Club). Youth Club theatres Krefeld and Mönchengladbach

19. – 21. 9. 2013
Sommerakademie *mies meets material – under construction* mit Studierenden der Bergischen Universität Wuppertal, der FH Aachen und der MSA Münster unter Leitung von Prof. Annette Hillebrandt
Online: www.fh-muenster.de/fb5/downloads/departments/schemel/mies_workshop.pdf

Mies & Muse, Veranstaltung der regionalen Kulturszene

20. 6. 2013
Doppelkonzert: Imbroglio und Horst Hansen Trio

27. 6. 2013
Lesung: Jahresfinale des *Papp a la Papp*-Poetry-Slams

1. 7. 2013
Lesung: *Ohrenschmaus. Vier Vorleser – Vier Bücher – Vergänglicher Ort!*

4. 7. 2013
Lesung: *Die verborgene Ordnung* mit Alfred van Cleef im Rahmen des 14. Literarischen Sommers

25. 7. 2013
Konzert: *Vue sur les jardins interdits*, Linos Saxophon Quartett

15. 8. 2013
Tanzperformance: *About Skys – Mies van der Rohe. Body – Architecture – City*. Kaiser Antonino and Guest Artists, Duisburg/Tel Aviv

22. 8. 2013
Konzert: *Mies 1:1 x 2insicht*

29. 8. 2013
Konzert: *Less is more,* phase : : vier

5. 9. 2013
Kabarett: *Spass satt* mit Volker Diefes und Michael C. Kent (Musik)

19. 9. 2013
Konzert: *Art of Voice goes Mies*. Vokalensemble

26. 9. 2013
Konzert: Mohammad Reza Mortazavi, Iran

27. – 29. 9. 2013
Installation: Peter Welz, Berlin. *Casa Malaparte – Mies [1:1 Golfclub]*

3. 10. 2013
Theaterstück: *Wir und der Golfclub (UA)*. Jugendclub des Theaters Krefeld und Mönchengladbach

Impressum/Colophon

© 2014 PROJEKT MIK, Krefeld
© 2014 für die Texte bei den Autoren
© 2014 für die Abbildungen bei Maarten Vanden Abeele,
Michael Dannenmann und Robbrecht en Daem architecten
© 2014 VG Bild-Kunst, Bonn für die Abbildungen von: Joachim Brohm,
Thomas Florschuetz, Ludwig Mies van der Rohe

Bildnachweis/Photo credit: Thomas Florschuetz: courtesy Galerie m Bochum;
Ludwig Mies van der Rohe: The Museum of Modern Art/Scala, Florence

Herausgeber/Editors:
  Christiane Lange, Robbrecht en Daem architecten
Gestaltung/Design:
  Neil Holt
Projektleitung/Managing editor:
  Nicola von Velsen
Lektorat/Copy-editors:
  Christine Fellhauer, Sarah Quigley
Übersetzung/Translations:
  Ted Alkins (J. und/and P. Robbrecht), Fiona Elliott (J. Heynen),
  Joseph Given (C. Lange, A. Schwarz),
  Stephan von Pohl (W. Speitkamp, R. Wendler),
  Klaus Roth (J. und/and P. Robbrecht)
Gesamtherstellung/Production:
  Lösch MedienManufaktur GmbH & Co. KG

Bibliografische Information der Deutschen Nationalbibliothek
Die Deutsche Nationalbibliothek verzeichnet diese Publikation in der
Deutschen Nationalbibliografie; detaillierte bibliografische Daten
sind über http://dnb.d-nb.de abrufbar.
  Bibliographic information published by the Deutsche Nationalbibliothek
The Deutsche Nationalbibliothek lists this publication in the Deutsche
Nationalbibliografie; detailed bibliographic data are available in the
Internet at http://dnb.d-nb.de.

  Vertrieb/Distribution:

Deutschland & Europa Germany & Europe
  Buchhandlung Walther König, Köln
  Ehrenstr. 4, 50672 Köln
  Tel. +49 (0) 221 / 20 59 6-53
  Fax +49 (0) 221 / 20 59 6-60
  verlag@buchhandlung-walther-koenig.de

Großbritannien & Irland/UK & Ireland
  Cornerhouse Publications
  70 Oxford Street
  GB-Manchester M1 5NH
  Fon +44 (0) 161 200 15 03
  Fax +44 (0) 161 200 15 04
  publications@cornerhouse.org

Außerhalb Europas/Outside Europe
  D.A.P./Distributed Art Publishers, Inc.
  155 6th Avenue, 2nd Floor
  USA-New York, NY 10013
  Fon +1 (0) 212 627 1999
  Fax +1 (0) 212 627 9484
  eleshowitz@dapinc.com

  ISBN 978-3-86335-644-6

  Printed in Germany

Maarten Vanden Abeele
photographs
of the 1:1 model

Maarten Vanden Abeele
Fotografien
des 1:1-Modells

3/3/2016